Introducing the Page: This activity may be used to introduce the pupil's text, or it may follow the first story. Have pupils circle the groups of seven items, and the word <u>seven</u> next to the scarecrow.

Additional Activity: Pupils may illustrate other situations in which the numeral <u>7</u> is significant.

Confrontation with uncertainties: Responding to illustrations

1

Compound Words

Put **X** on the line if the word is a compound word.

_____ gingerbread

_____ had

_____ shaving

_____ into

_____ sometimes

_____ baseball

_____ face

_____ children

_____ grasshopper

Make these compound words into 2 words. Draw a line
as you see here: **air/port**

w i t h o u t	**b e a n b a g**
p o l i c e m a n	**S u n d a y**
g r a n d m o t h e r	**o u t s i d e**
p a r k w a y	**s n o w m a n**

Draw a line from a word in **Side A** to a word in **Side B**
to make a compound word.

A	**B**
in	thing
some	port
air	bal!
snow	side

Structural analysis: Compound words

Introducing the Page: Help pupils read the words compound, word, draw.

Additional Activity: Pupils may illustrate the two parts in each of the following: snowball, firemen, beanbag, snowman. Let pupils determine the compound words illustrated by their classmates.

People You Know

Find the words that go in the blanks. Write them. The pictures will help you!

shook   **took**   **hook**   **wood**

good   **Look**   **book**   **hood**

_____

‑ ‑ ‑ ‑ ‑ ‑ ‑ ‑ ‑ ‑ ‑

_____ at Mike!

_____

‑ ‑ ‑ ‑ ‑ ‑ ‑ ‑ ‑ ‑ ‑

He has on a new _____ .

Mother gave Pat a box.

_____

‑ ‑ ‑ ‑ ‑ ‑ ‑ ‑ ‑ ‑ ‑

He _____ it up and down.

_____

‑ ‑ ‑ ‑ ‑ ‑ ‑ ‑ ‑ ‑ ‑

Carlo goes fishing on _____ days.

_____

‑ ‑ ‑ ‑ ‑ ‑ ‑ ‑ ‑ ‑ ‑

On bad days he stays in and reads a _____ .

_____

‑ ‑ ‑ ‑ ‑ ‑ ‑ ‑ ‑ ‑ ‑

Dad wanted some _____ .

_____

‑ ‑ ‑ ‑ ‑ ‑ ‑ ‑ ‑ ‑ ‑

Pat _____ some out of the shed.

Introducing the Page: Point out the graphemic base <u>ook</u> in <u>cook</u> and <u>book</u>. Have pupils name other words with the same base. Help pupils read the words <u>blanks</u>, <u>words</u>.

Additional Activity: Have pupils use as many of the words as possible from the top of the page in original stories.

Phonemic and structural analysis: Correspondence /u/<u>oo</u>, graphemic base <u>ook</u>

3

Introducing the Page: Ask pupils for comments on family snapshot albums containing their own pictures over a period of time. Relate their comments to this page.

Additional Activity: Pupils may make picture books with illustrations of themselves showing how they have changed from babyhood. Others may wish to bring pictures to school from home.

Jeff's mother has a picture book.

In it are pictures of Jeff.

Make a picture of Jeff when he was little.

When Jeff was five, he went to school.

Make a picture of Jeff on his way to school.

When Jeff was six, he got a bike.

Make a picture of Jeff on his bike.

Now Jeff's mother will take a new picture.

Can you guess what the new picture will be?

Literal comprehension: Recognizing and recalling details

Riddles

Find the word for the riddle. Write it on the line.

smear   **Smith**   **smell**   **smile**   **smack**

I may come from hot gingerbread, but you will not see me.

_____

I am a _____.

Sometimes you can see me.
Sometimes you can't.
This boy can see me.

_____

I am a _____.

I am in ball games.
You may hear me when the bat hits the ball.

_____

I am a _____.

Some people do not want me.
I am a mess.

_____

I am a _____.

Phonemic analysis: Correspondence /sm/**sm**

5

You Hear Sounds

Read these words. If you hear the same sound as in **Sam** and **sit,** write the word under **Sam**. If you hear the same sound as in **keep** and **Kay**, write the word under **keep**.

	Sam	keep
call		
face		
came		
cap		
city		
car		
come		
nice		
Lucy		
can't		
Carlo		

Introducing the Page: Write Sam and keep. Ask pupils which of the two initial sounds they hear in country and city. Write country under keep and city under Sam. Call attention to the initial sounds. Help pupils read the words word, sound, write.

Additional Activity: Have pupils look through the first three stories of the text for words in which the letter c stands for the initial sound in city or country. Let them classify these words under city or country.

Phonemic analysis: Correspondences /s/c (medial), /s/ce, /s/ci, /k/c

Little Words

Find the word that fits the sentence. Write it on the line.

He   **her**   **It**   **She**   **his**   **him**

Pat wanted _____ picture with the others.

Pat's dad gave _____ this picture.

Mike has a new book.

_____ is about animals.

_____ can read the book.

Jill wants to ride in _____ dad's car.

_____ likes to ride in the country.

Word meaning: Using pronouns

Additional Activity: Pupils may think of and challenge each other with sentences similar to the first sentence on the page in which the missing pronoun must be supplied.

Introducing the Page: Help pupils read the words sentence, write, word.

"Lucy's Smile," 17–22   •   Teachers' Edition, 49–55

What Do You Hear?

In 2 words in the line, the sound that <u>o</u> stands for will be the same.

Circle the 2 words.

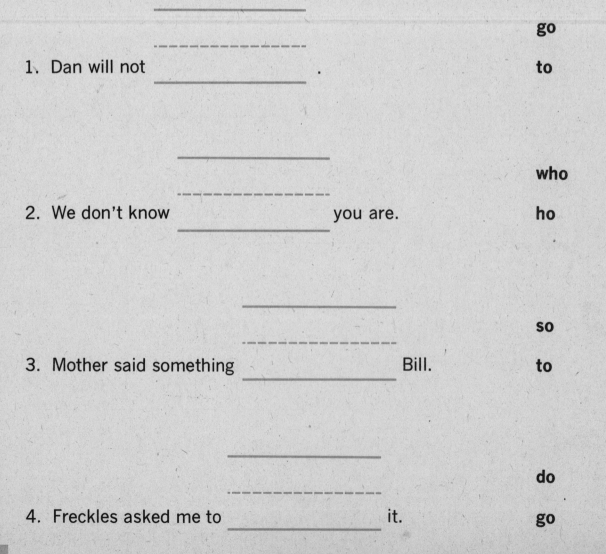

1.	n<u>o</u>	g<u>o</u>	t<u>o</u>
2.	s<u>o</u>	t<u>o</u>	<u>o</u>h
3.	d<u>o</u>n't	<u>o</u>n	n<u>o</u>
4.	tr<u>o</u>ll	wh<u>o</u>	d<u>o</u>
5.	Carl<u>o</u>	t<u>o</u>	s<u>o</u>
6.	g<u>o</u>	wh<u>o</u>	n<u>o</u>

Pick the word that goes on the line. Write the word.

1. Dan will not _____ .   **go**
                                                        to

2. We don't know _____ you are.   **who**
                                                        ho

3. Mother said something _____ Bill.   **so**
                                                        to

4. Freckles asked me to _____ it.   **do**
                                                        go

Phonemic analysis: Correspondences /uw/<u>o</u> /ow/<u>o</u>

"The Magic in Seven," 23–28 • Teachers' Edition, 56–62

Introducing the Page: Help pupils read the words circle, sound, stands, words.

Additional Activity: Pupils may use in written sentences the words which were not selected to fill the blanks in the second part of the page.

What Did Bill Do?

Check the right answer.

My name is **Bill**.

What did Bill do?

_____ Match the words.

_____ Check the answer.

_____ Finish the sentence.

I am a _____.

boy   plan   picture

What did Bill do?

_____ Underline the answer.

_____ Draw a picture.

_____ Circle the right word.

Dogs can be pets.

Hats   Chops   Dogs

What did Bill do?

_____ Do a puzzle.

_____ Fill in the blank.

_____ Pick the best ending.

---

book

(k)   p   m

What did Bill do?

_____ Circle the best ending for a story.

_____ Circle a letter that stands for a sound.

Word meaning: Understanding direction words

9

Additional Activity: Have pupils copy on a piece of paper each of these directions and carry out the directions on the paper: 1. Draw a circle. 2. Draw a line. 3. Make a check. 4. Underline a sentence. 5. Write a word.

Introducing the Page: Explain to pupils that Bill had four things to do on this page, and that they must figure out which set of directions Bill followed in each case. Help pupils read the words right, answer.

Find the Answers

Pick the letters that go on the line. Write them.

grade

1. My brother is in the 4th _____ ade.

trade

_____

2. What is on that _____ ay?

tray

stay

_____

3. Mike hit the building with a _____ ick.

trick

stick

_____

4. Can you _____ im the tree?

grim

trim

_____

5. Carlo rides his bike down the _____ ack.

track

stack

_____

6. What _____ ate do you live in?

grate

state

_____

7. Where did Lucy _____ ay?

stay

gray

_____

8. I will _____ ade my ball for that kite.

grade

trade

Phonemic analysis: Correspondences /gr/**gr**, /tr/**tr**, /st/**st**

Introducing the Page: Help pupils read the words letters, write.

Additional Activity: Pupils may illustrate other items beginning with clusters gr, tr, or st, and label their pictures with the appropriate cluster.

What Do You Think?

Circle the right answer.

Andy went to the store.

He got fish and milk.

He took them to Grandmother.

1. What did Andy get?

fish and cream   milk and cream   fish and milk

2. Who did Andy go to the store for?

Father   Grandfather   Grandmother

3. Where did Andy take the food?

to the store   to Grandmother   to the country

A man came to Jill's house.

He put in a new telephone.

The new telephone is red.

1. Who came to Jill's house?

Jill   a boy   a man

2. The new telephone is _ _ _ _ _ _ _ .

old   red   green

3. Where is the new telephone?

in the man's house   in Jill's house   in Bill's house

Literal comprehension: Recalling story details

Can You Do This at School?

Make an **X** under **YES** if you can do this at school.

Make an **X** under **NO** if you can't.

	YES	NO

If you are in school, can you . . .

1. read books about lions?

2. ride in cars?

3. go fishing?

4. make pictures?

5. see other children?

6. go for a swim?

7. trap animals?

8. get some shaving cream?

9. go to sleep?

10. ride on a bridge?

11. answer a telephone?

12. dig a well?

13. see seven faces?

14. be 4th in line?

Literal comprehension: Classifying ideas

Introducing the Page: Pupils should understand that answers may vary.

Additional Activity: Have pupils substitute outside or in a car for the words in school. They may then answer the questions once again with another color.

Draw a line under the word that tells about the picture.

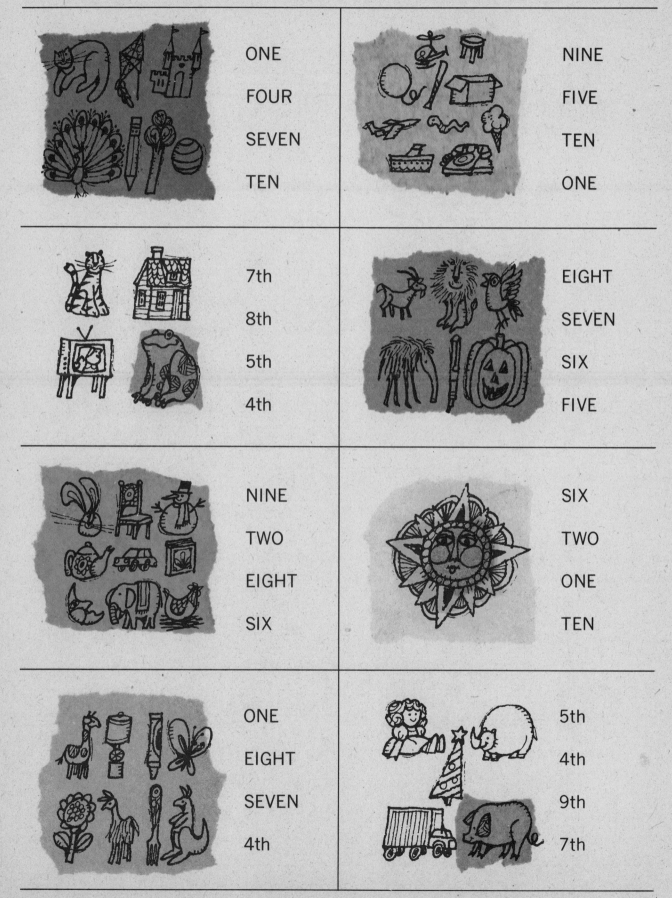

ONE
FOUR
SEVEN
TEN

NINE
FIVE
TEN
ONE

7th
8th
5th
4th

EIGHT
SEVEN
SIX
FIVE

NINE
TWO
EIGHT
SIX

SIX
TWO
ONE
TEN

ONE
EIGHT
SEVEN
4th

5th
4th
9th
7th

Word meaning: Understanding cardinal and ordinal numbers

Helping with a Story

How will the sentence end? Underline the answer.

1.

"Come with me, Lucy," said Ted.

"We can go _____."

to the zoo   **on the zoo**

2.

Lucy and Ted ran all the way.

They ran _____.

with the street   **down the street**

3.

"This is fun!" said Ted.

"Here we are _____."

under the zoo   **at the zoo**

4.

A policeman saw the children.

He waved _____.

down them   **to them**

5.

"Look at that lion!" said Ted.

"There is a smile _____."

on his face   **to his face**

6.

"Let's telephone home," said Lucy.

"Mother will want to know _____."

where we are   **when we are**

Syntactical understanding: Completing sentences with the appropriate phrase

A Puzzle for You

Read the words and sentences.   Pick the words for the puzzle.   Write them in.

chill

chin

children

chap

chip

chops

cheeks

check

ACROSS

4. It is the same as <u>boys and girls</u>.

DOWN

1. You may be sick if you have one.

2. You have two on your face.

3. Do you like to eat pork_____?

Phonemic analysis: Correspondence /č/<u>ch</u> in initial position

Introducing the Page: Pupils may need an explanation of the procedure for completing a crossword puzzle.
Help pupils read the words sentence, puzzle, across, <u>word</u>.

Then What?

Read the first 2 sentences of the story. Write **3** on the line

for the sentence that finishes the story.

__1__ Mother wanted some milk.

__2__ She asked Ted to go to the store.

_____ She got cream from the store.

_____ Ted remembered to get the milk.

__1__ Lucy had a birthday.

__2__ She got a new book from Grandmother.

_____ Lucy likes to read her new book.

_____ Lucy hasn't seen her brother yet.

__1__ Mike answered the telephone.

__2__ "Did you remember that it was Grandmother's birthday?" Dad asked.

_____ "There aren't any fish in the store," said Mrs. Dandy.

_____ "I remembered," answered Mike. "I have something for her."

__1__ Mr. King couldn't make his car go.

__2__ Mr. King asked Ted to telephone the store.

_____ Mr. King asked Ted for a birthday cake.

_____ Ted called to get help for Mr. King.

Inferential comprehension: Inferring sequence

Introducing the Page: Help pupils read the words write, sentence, story.

Additional Activity: Pupils may illustrate one of the little stories in a three-part comic strip.

What Do You See?

Circle the word that tells about the picture.

today birthday sometimes	chops apartment children	school so shaving	wasn't waved well
smile four face	grandmothers others brothers	about answers apartments	magic maybe milk
answer remember telephone	seven milk cream	king couldn't keep	his well hamster
picture pork took	fire fish face	Mr. White Lucy Miss White	pork chops milk sometimes

Word recognition: Identifying new words through picture associations

Additional Activity: Pupils may make cards for at least six words on the page including any words they missed. Have them write the word on one side of the card and illustrate it on the other side. Let pupils try to name the words by looking at the illustrations. They may work together.

Introducing the Page: Help pupils read the words circle, word.

"Pork Chops and Applesauce," 35–40 • Teachers' Edition, 72–80

Can You Do It?

Underline the word that fits best in the sentence.

1. Did someone _____ the eggs?

   cook   **cheat**

2. Dan likes to _____ his cars.

   hook   **race**

3. Do you eat _____?

   hood   **rice**

4. Did Carlo find the _____?

   place   **chill**

5. I _____ the 4th box.

   smiled   **shook**

6. I see red _____ on Mother's hat.

   mice   **lace**

7. My _____ is on my face.

   chin   **chill**

8. Kay baked _____ .

   hooks   **rolls**

9. Everything looks so _____ .

   nice   **5th**

10. He will _____ everyone.

    chase   **smile**

Evaluation: Decoding

Introducing the Page: Help pupils read the words <u>underline</u>, <u>best</u>, <u>word</u>, <u>sentence</u>.

For Individual Needs: See Teachers' Edition—compounds—38, 47; /u̇/oo and ook—46, 83; /sm/sm—53, 55, 81, 83; /s/c—53, 83; /ow/o—61; /č/ch (initial)—77, 81, 83.

Read this story.

Don't you like to see people smile?

Some people smile when they work.

We may smile when we play.

Do you smile when you read a funny book?

Make this boy smile!

Write the answers.

1. What do you like to see people do?

   _____

   _____

   _____

2. Some people smile when they

   _____

   _____

   _____ .

3. We may smile when we

   _____

   _____

   _____ .

   _____

   _____

4. A _____ book may make you smile.

   _____

   _____

5. Do you have a _____ on your face?

Evaluation for Unit 1 • • • Teacher's Edition, 83–84

For Individual Needs: To gain insight into pupils' problems with recognizing and recalling details, meet with each pupil on an individual basis, have the passage and questions read aloud, and the answers discussed.

Introducing the Page: Help pupils read the word story. Ask pupils to tell what they think these sentences will be about. Tell them that they will learn from the story what they should draw on the face.

Evaluation: Literal Comprehension

Find the Word

Circle the word that tells about the picture.

face	telephone	have
apartment	tales	white
fish	thought	waves

brothers	birthday	white
children	balloons	kite
girls	building	well

one	smile	milk
four	shaving	chops
seven	street	fish

Evaluation: Vocabulary Development

Introducing the Page: Have the directions read aloud.

For Individual Needs: So that other exercises may be prepared for those who have not yet developed the ability to recognize new words in Unit 1, refer to page 237 of the pupil's text for a list of all words introduced in this unit.

Can You Find the Word?

One of the 3 words will be right for the sentence. Circle the word.

1. Mike _ _ _ _ _ _ _ _ _ _ _ a book out of the box.

   picked   **lived**   **backed**

_____

2. Dan _ _ _ _ _ _ _ _ _ _ up the pictures.

   smiled   **mixed**   **milked**

_____

3. She _ _ _ _ _ _ _ _ _ _ her car into that building.

   waited   **backed**   **named**

_____

4. No one _ _ _ _ _ _ _ _ _ _ him when he called.

   mailed   **looked**   **answered**

_____

5. Everything looked white after it _ _ _ _ _ _ _ _ _ _ .

   snowed   **shaved**   **named**

_____

6. Lucy _ _ _ _ _ _ _ _ _ _ everyone for her birthday surprise.

   stayed   **thanked**   **backed**

_____

7. Do you know what Ann _ _ _ _ _ _ _ _ _ _ her cat?

   named   **fished**   **snowed**

_____

8. Ken and Dad _ _ _ _ _ _ _ _ _ _ a game.

   answered   **played**   **milked**

_____

9. That little boy _ _ _ _ _ _ _ _ _ _ them to the park.

   followed   **smiled**   **parked**

_____

Structural analysis: Verbs with inflections **ed** and **d**

Additional Activity: Pupils may write on small cards the words that were not used in the sentences. Small groups of children may devise games involving these cards.

Introducing the Page: Have pupils use the following words in oral sentences: answered, fished, faced, mailed, remembered, shaved. Help pupils realize that the words all refer to a completed action, and that this past tense is signaled by the inflection _d_ or _ed_.

The School Fair

Underline the best ending for the story.

Bill liked to work at the fair.
He helped Mr. Mays with the food.
It looked so good!
Bill wanted to help, and he
wanted . . .

to run away.

to eat the good things.

to go home.

Kay and Jill were on the steps.
They could see Bill working.
They could see Bozo too.
It was fun to have . . .

a new book to read.

lions at the fair.

a fair at Anders School.

Bozo was working, but he had
fun too.
He did some tricks for the
children.
Bozo liked to make the
children . . .

work at the fair.

smile at his tricks.

pet the lions.

The fair lasted all day.
When night came, Mr. Mays and
the others still had work to do.
They had to . . .

eat all the food.

see Bozo's tricks.

put all the things away.

Inferential comprehension: Predicting story endings

The Contents Page

Answer the questions that are under this Contents page.

CONTENTS

ONE

On Top of a Lion 7

Bob Finds a Pal 10

Rock City 15

The Fox and the Hog 19

TWO

Bozo's Job 24

A Parking Lot 28

Men at the Docks 31

The Green Socks 37

On what page in Part Two is the story about something for a boy's feet? _____

On what page in Part One is the story about one animal? _____

On what page in Part Two is the story about cars? _____

On what page in Part One is the story about a boy who meets someone? _____

"Kay," 48–54 • Teachers' Edition, 94–101

Introducing the Page: Have pupils look at the Contents pages of their books to examine the parts of a Contents page. Relate their comments to this activity. Help pupils read the words contents, story, questions.

Additional Activity: Have the children think of a title for a book that might have this Contents page. They may design covers for the "book" and write their titles on the covers.

Phonemic analysis: Correspondence /a/o

Make a Word

Pick the words that fit in the sentences. You may pick
a word just one time. Write the missing letter on the line.

Tall

call

wall

caw

saw

1. Kay made a small yellow book.

   The children __ aw it.

   "What will we __ all it?" said Bill.

   "Do you like the name ' __ all Trees'?" asked Lucy.

calls

halls

fall

caw

ball

paw

2. Ted __ alls his dog King.

   King puts out his __ aw to say "Hello."

   One day Ted gave a __ all to King.

   King just let the ball __ all.

saw

call

ball

paw

wall

3. "I don't know what to call my cat," said Dan.

   "Why don't you __ all him Snowball?" asked Jack.

   "I thought of it when I __ aw him."

   "He just looks like a __ all of snow!"

24

Phonemic analysis: /ɔ/a, /ɔ/aw Structural analysis: all

Introducing the Page: Have the directions read aloud. Note any pupil who has difficulty with these direction words. He may need some additional help at a later time.

Additional Activity: Pupils may use in written sentences those words which were not selected as responses.

Stop and Think

Check the best ending for the story.

1. Kay mailed the postcard to the Anders School.

   She mailed a yellow book too.

   The children at Anders School liked _ _ _ _ _ _ _ _ _ _ .

   _____ **to make boxes**   _____ **the surprise that Kay made**

2. A lumberman works in the woods.

   He puts tags on the trees.

   He tags the trees _ _ _ _ _ _ _ _ _ _ .

   _____ **that will be cut**   _____ **that will be sawmills**

3. Some men put logs on trucks.

   The trucks take the logs away.

   The logs go _ _ _ _ _ _ _ _ _ _ .

   _____ **to feed the fish**   _____ **to a sawmill**

4. Logs are cut in a sawmill.

   They come from the log pond.

   Saws cut the logs into _ _ _ _ _ _ _ _ _ _ .

   _____ **lumber**   _____ **lumbermen**

5. Houses can be made from lumber.

   Things we see every day are made from wood.

   Some of these things are _ _ _ _ _ _ _ _ _ _ .

   _____ **book cases and beds**   _____ **ponds and people**

Inferential comprehension: Predicting outcomes

"Kay," 48–54 • Teachers' Edition, 94–101

Introducing the Page: Have pupils cite situations in which they, or people they know, have tried to predict the outcome to a situation. Explain that pupils will be making predictions on this page. Help pupils read the words story, best, ending.

What Do You Think about This?

Underline all the endings that seem right to you.

A new fence _ _ _ _ _ _ _ _ _ _ .

could be white   could be made of logs

can be made of wood   could have snow on it

can answer you   can read a book

In an apartment you could find _ _ _ _ _ _ _ _ _ _ .

big animals   new and old pictures

logs for a fire   an airport

green grass   books to read

Jack and Bill would like to _ _ _ _ _ _ _ _ _ _ .

play house   stay inside all the time

ride on a jet   have 2 telephones

play ball   take a nap every day

You could find fish _ _ _ _ _ _ _ _ _ _ .

in a store   under the bed

on a red plate   on a tall tree

in a big pond   in a lake

Entertaining improbabilities: Distinguishing reality from fantasy

"Kay," 48–54 • Teachers' Edition, 94–101

Introducing the Page: Explain to pupils that they may underline every answer which seems sensible to them, and that any answer which they can justify will be acceptable.

Additional Activity: Have pupils change the words fence to book, apartment to zoo, Jack and Bill to Lucy and Kay, and fish to logs, and underline their new responses in another color.

Do You Know What These Words Mean?

Draw a line from the words in **Side A**
to the words in **Side B** that mean the same thing.

Side A	Side B
to give	to mend
to send letters	to mail
to fix	to hand over

Read the sentences. Write the letters that go on the lines.

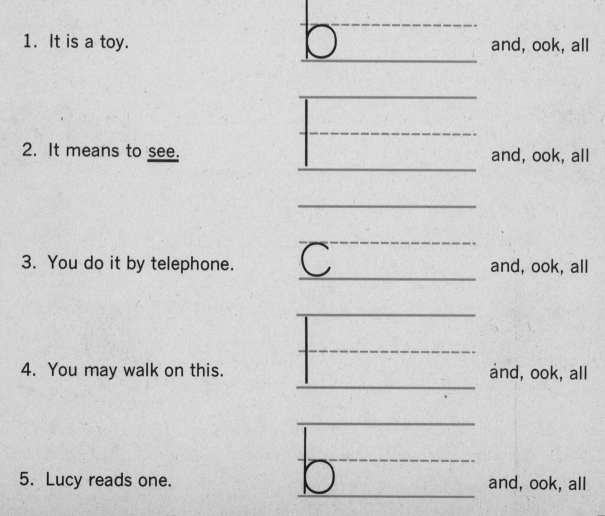

1. It is a toy. b _ _ _ _ _ _   and, ook, all

2. It means to <u>see</u>. l _ _ _ _ _ _   and, ook, all

3. You do it by telephone. c _ _ _ _ _ _   and, ook, all

4. You may walk on this. l _ _ _ _ _ _   and, ook, all

5. Lucy reads one. b _ _ _ _ _ _   and, ook, all

Words That Work

Write the word on the line.

face   **park**   **cream**   **Mike**   **whistle**

This is _____. This is too!

This has a _____. She has one too.

Mike can _____. This is one too!

This is _____. This is one.

Additional Activity: Have pupils draw two pictures for each of the following words: bat, pen, sheet, tracks. The pictures should show two meanings for each word.

Word meaning: Using words in more than one way

Make a Postcard

This looks just like a postcard. Can you fill it in?

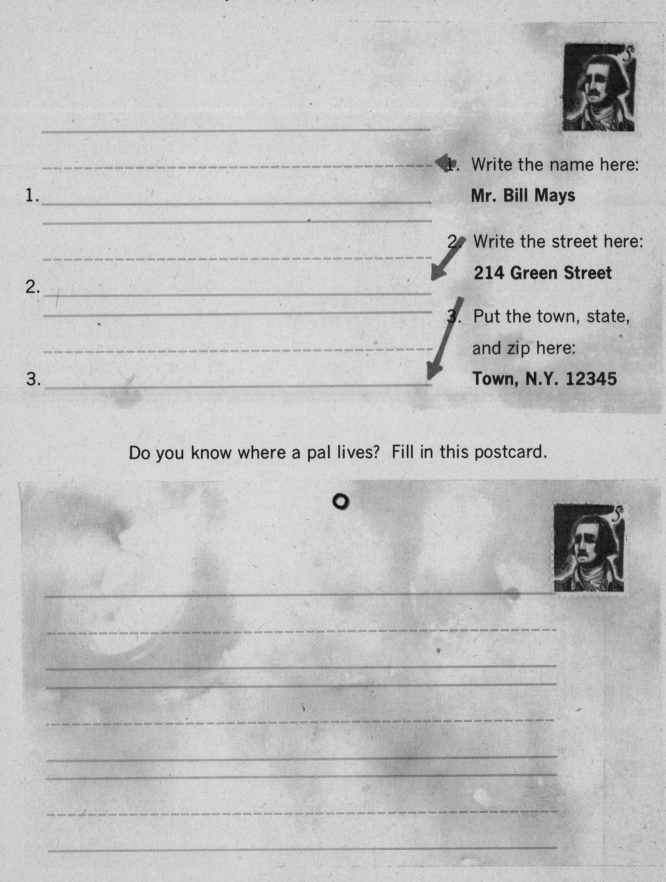

1. _____

2. _____

3. _____

1. Write the name here:
Mr. Bill Mays

2. Write the street here:
214 Green Street

3. Put the town, state, and zip here:
Town, N.Y. 12345

Do you know where a pal lives? Fill in this postcard.

Now turn this page.

"A Balloon That Works," 55–57 • Teachers' Edition, 102–110

Introducing the Page: Have the directions read aloud for this page and the next. Pupils may separate into pairs and work together.

Write a postcard to a pal. Then check it.

Dear _____,

Now write it on this postcard. Cut out the postcard.

Hang the postcard so that others may see it.

o

"A Balloon That Works," 55-57 • Teachers' Edition, 102-110

Introducing the Page: Tell pupils that you will suspend a string so that they may exhibit their finished postcards.

Additional Activity: Pupils may add to the postcard display with signs telling about postcards. They may include also actual postcards of their own showing the variety of types and sizes of postcards.

Writing skills: Addressing and writing postcards

Think about It

Pick the word that fits in the sentence. Write it on the line.

Additional Activity: Have pupils illustrate and label illustrations with the following words: hand, sand, wind, plant, tent, band.

_____

_ up!

_____

Mend

Stand

_____

_ _ _ _ _ _ _ _ _ _ _ _ _ _ _ _ _ _ _

His dad plays in the _____ .

band

mend

_____

_ _ _ _ _ _ _ _ _ _ _ _ _ _ _ _ _ _ _

May I _____ this letter to Mike?

sand

send

_____

_ _ _ _ _ _ _ _ _ _ _ _ _ _ _ _ _ _ _

Do jets _____ at the airport?

band

land

_____

_ _ _ _ _ _ _ _ _ _ _ _ _ _ _ _ _ _ _

Why did Carlo _____ over?

wind

bend

_____

_ _ _ _ _ _ _ _ _ _ _ _ _ _ _ _ _ _ _

That's a fine green _____ you have there!

went

plant

_____

_ _ _ _ _ _ _ _ _ _ _ _ _ _ _ _ _ _ _

Lucy asked for a _____ about her surprise.

vent

hint

_____

_ _ _ _ _ _ _ _ _ _ _ _ _ _ _ _ _ _ _

The boys will stay in a _____ .

bent

tent

_____

_ _ _ _ _ _ _ _ _ _ _ _ _ _ _ _ _ _ _

He _____ his pal a postcard.

sent

bent

"Sky House," 62–66 • Teachers' Edition, 112–119

Phonemic analysis: Correspondences /nd/**nd,** /nt/**nt** in final position

It's a Puzzle

Read a sentence. Find the word it tells about.

Write the missing letters in the puzzle.

hood	zoo
school	hoop
books	food
roof	took
moon	spoon
shook	woods
balloon	stool

ACROSS

2. You may put this on when you go outside.

3. This may be a toy, or it may do work.

5. Where do some animals live?

6. What may you eat with?

7. Where do many children go to work and play?

DOWN

1. What may you see in the sky at night?

2. This can be a toy.

3. You can read these.

4. This is on the top of a house.

"Sky House," 62–66 • Teachers' Edition, 112–119

Introducing the Page: Help pupils read the word puzzle. Review with pupils the procedure for completing a crossword puzzle. Refer to the puzzle on page 15 as a reminder of the procedure.

Phonemic analysis: Correspondences /uw/oo, /u/oo

Pictures and Sounds

Think of a word that tells about the picture. Circle the letters that stand for the sound you hear at the end of the words.

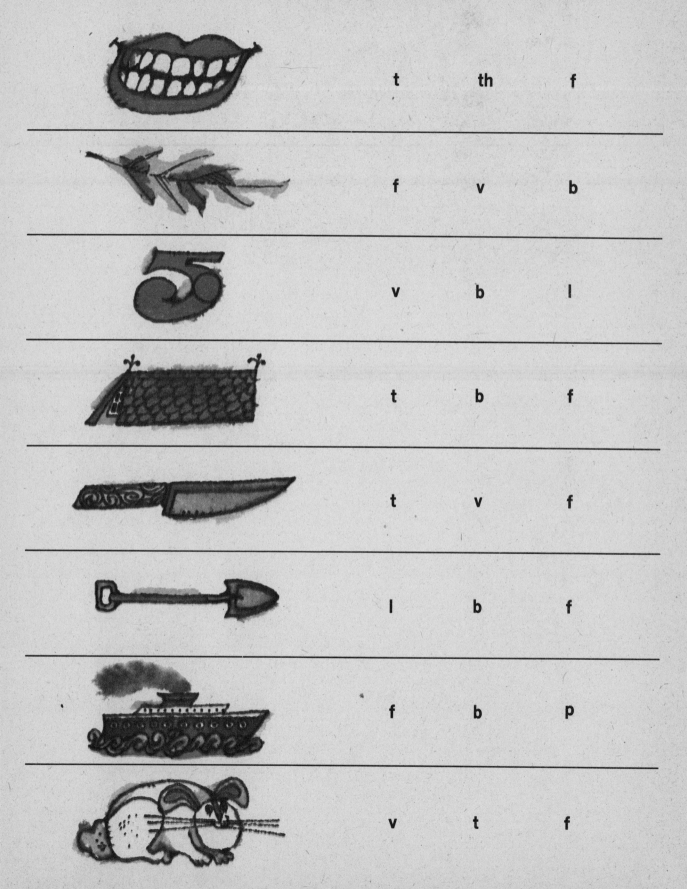

t	th	f
f	v	b
v	b	l
t	b	f
t	v	f
l	b	f
f	b	p
v	t	f

Additional Activity: Have pupils illustrate three other words with the same ending sound as knife or roof.

"Sky House," 62–66 • Teachers' Edition, 112–119

Introducing the Page: Call attention to the words stand, sound, end, circle.

Phonemic analysis: Correspondence /f/ f in final position

LOTS OF THOUGHTS

There are things to see
Like machines and shells.
There are things to hear
Like whistles and bells.

But then I read words
Like **took** and **tall**
That I can't see . . . .

or hear . . . .

at all!

"Air Mail," 67–71 • Teachers' Edition, 120–127

Introducing the Page: Have pupils read "Lots of Thoughts" silently. Then select a child to read it aloud. Relate pupils' comments to the remainder of the page.

Additional Activity: Have pupils illustrate some other things which they may SEE OR HEAR.

Write the words that tell what you can SEE OR HEAR
in one list. Write under OTHER THINGS the words
that tell what you can't see or hear.

	SEE OR HEAR	OTHER THINGS
pot		
got		
boxes		
fox		
hot		
doll		
on		
not		

Phonemic analysis: Correspondence /a/**o**

Think about This

Put an **X** on the right pictures.

Additional Activity: Have pupils draw one additional correct response for each of the three questions.

Can it go up in the air?

Can it come to you in the mail?

Can you see it from the roof?

"Air Mail," 67–71 • Teachers' Edition, 120–127

Literal comprehension: Classifying ideas

You Can Make Words

Write __OO__ in the blanks. Then make a line from the
word to the picture it tells about.

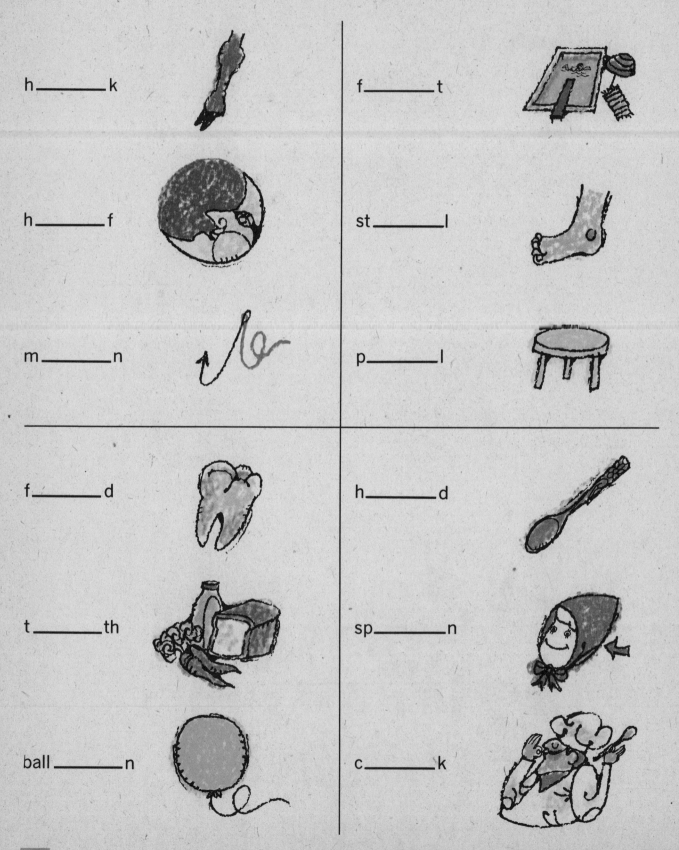

h_____k

h_____f

m_____n

f_____d

t_____th

ball_____n

f_____t

st_____l

p_____l

h_____d

sp_____n

c_____k

Phonemic analysis: Correspondences /u/ oo, /uw/ oo

"More about Balloons," 73–76 • Teachers' Edition, 129–136

Introducing the Page: Write on the chalkboard s __ n, t __ k, sch __ l, l __ k. Have pupils fil in the blanks with the letters oo and read the words they have completed.

Additional Activity: Write the following words on the chalkboard for pupils to copy and illustrate: cookbook, bedroom, toothpick, football.

Who Am I?

Find my name, and write it on the line.

jet	basket	telephone	balloon
smile	postcard	birthday	fire

I am little.

I can be mailed.

You can read me.

I am a

_____

- - - - - - - - - - - - - - - -

_____ .

All people have one.

I come one time a year.

I can be fun for boys and girls.

I am a

_____

- - - - - - - - - - - - - - - -

_____ .

You can make calls on me.

I may be in a house.

I'm not big.

I am a

_____

- - - - - - - - - - - - - - - -

_____ .

I can be a toy.

I can do work too.

I can let you know about weather.

I am a

_____

- - - - - - - - - - - - - - - -

_____ .

I am hot.

I can help you in many ways.

You have to be careful with me.

I am

_____

- - - - - - - - - - - - - - - -

_____

I can fly fast.

I can go up into space.

People can ride in me.

I am a

_____

- - - - - - - - - - - - - - - -

_____

"More about Balloons," 73–76 • Teachers' Edition, 129–136

Additional Activity: Have pupils use the leftover words at the top of the page in an original story. They need not use every word in their stories.

Introducing the Page: Have pupils offer their definitions for the word riddle. Relate their comments to the page.

Inferential comprehension: Deducing an answer from descriptive clues

Words and Pictures

Underline the word that names the picture.

thinks	turtle	lumber
things	tree	logs
telephone	truck	lake
weather	snow	postcard
workers	smile	people
woman	smoke	picture
sky	pan	Mike
shave	pond	milk
snow	postcard	met

Word recognition: Identifying new words through picture association

Additional Activity: Have pupils illustrate one of the other words in each exercise, labeling each illustration with that word.

Are You Ready for a Dictionary?

Write **1** in the blank for the word that would come first in the dictionary.

Then write **2** for the word that would follow the first one.

Write **3** for the word that would come last.

_____ brother	_____ king	_____ thought
_____ apartment	_____ jump	_____ sky
_____ chops	_____ logs	_____ under
_____ day	_____ space	_____ far
_____ before	_____ ride	_____ Don
_____ children	_____ tags	_____ every
_____ night	_____ picture	_____ weather
_____ my	_____ quack	_____ under
_____ off	_____ right	_____ van
_____ fair	_____ leaf	_____ pork
_____ helicopter	_____ know	_____ other
_____ grandmother	_____ just	_____ name
_____ sawmill	_____ go	_____ Kay
_____ trucks	_____ in	_____ more
_____ roof	_____ had	_____ letter

Locational skills: Alphabetizing words

"More about Balloons," 73–76 • Teachers' Edition, 129–136
Introducing the Page: Help pupils read the word dictionary. Have some picture dictionaries on hand for pupils to examine. Do the first exercise with the group.

Can You Match Them?

Match the word and its meaning. The first one
has been answered for you.

1. **socks**   _____ penny

2. **wall**   _____ a kind of meat

3. **cent**   _____ the side of a house

4. **beef**   **1** things for feet

1. **pool**   _____ a name for a boy

2. **Bob**   _____ something to sit on

3. **stool**   _____ something to swim in

1. **tent**   _____ this may fall from a tree

2. **leaf**   _____ something to sleep in outside

3. **fox**   _____ some work

4. **job**   _____ a kind of animal

Evaluation: Decoding

Evaluation for Unit 2 • Teachers' Edition, 139-141

Introducing the Page: Have the directions read aloud. Help pupils read the word match.

For Individual Needs: See Teachers' Edition—/ɔ/ a, /ɔ/ aw, all—99, 124, 137, 139, 140; /a/ o—99, 124, 137, 139; /nd/ nd, and—105, 107, 139; /nt/ nt—116; /f/ f (final)—117; /uw/ oo—116, 126, 133, 139.

Some Riddles for Fun

Underline the answer.

1. I can be made of wood.

    You can put things to eat in me.

    You may take me to the park.

    I am a _____ .

    pan   basket   sky

2. I can go up in the air.

    I may be filled with air too.

    You may like to play with me.

    I am a _____ .

    basket   sky   balloon

3. Mother may have one.

    She may fix good things to eat in me.

    I am a _____ .

    letter   fire   pan

4. You have to look up to see me.

    Helicopters and jets fly up into me.

    I am the _____ .

    basket   sky   balloon

5. Sometimes I am good.

    Sometimes I am bad.

    I am good when I make you warm.

    I am _____ .

    letter   fire   pan

Evaluation: Inferential Comprehension

For Individual Needs: Meet individually with pupils who have difficulty deducing responses from specific clues. Have the exercises read aloud and responses discussed.

Evaluation for Unit 2 • Teachers' Edition, 139–141
Introducing the Page: Help pupils recall what a riddle is. Relate their comments to this page.

Can You Finish These?

Check the best answer.

1. Mike got some red balloons.

   He wanted to put air _ _ _ _ _ _ _ _ _ _ .

   ___ **on the balloons**   ___ **into the balloons**

   ___ **under the balloons**

2. Bill had a new green kite.

   He wanted the kite to go _ _ _ _ _ _ _ _ _ _ .

   ___ **over the tree**   ___ **under the tree**

   ___ **into the tree**

3. Nan looked for her red boots.

   She saw them _ _ _ _ _ _ _ _ _ _ .

   ___ **into the toy box**   ___ **over the toy box**

   ___ **in the toy box**

4. Kay wanted to go to Grandmother's house.

   She put something to eat _ _ _ _ _ _ _ _ _ _ .

   ___ **along a basket**   ___ **in a basket**

   ___ **over a basket**

5. Ted saw a funny, little dog.

   The dog jumped around _ _ _ _ _ _ _ _ _ _ .

   ___ **before the grass**   ___ **in the grass**

   ___ **with the grass**

Evaluation for Unit 2 • Teachers' Edition, 139–141
Introducing the Page: Have the directions read aloud.

For Individual Needs: Meet on an individual basis with any pupil who has difficulty with syntactical understanding. Have the pupil give reasons for his response. As he reads the exercises and speaks about his responses, his problem may be pinpointed.

Evaluation: Language Development

What's Missing?

Look at the picture. Write one of the letters in the blank so that the word tells about the picture.

a e i u

c ____ p	tr ____ ck	p ____ g
d ____ ck	t ____ n	j ____ t
b ____ g	n ____ t	b ____ g
w ____ b	b ____ s	r ____ g
s ____ n	p ____ n	m ____ p
b ____ d	f ____ n	l ____ g
j ____ m	b ____ ll	t ____ b

Phonemic analysis: Correspondences /æ/**a**, /e/**e**, /i/**i**, /ə/**u**

The Talking Dog

Finish the words that fit in the sentences. Pick from these words.

band   **p**aw   **t**alk   **b**all   **h**all   **t**all   **t**ook   **h**and

Mike thought he could make Sandy talk.

"If I put out my **h**_____ , he will **t**_____ ."

Mike put out his **h**_____ , but Sandy just looked at him.

Then Ted said, "He will **t**_____ , if I let him get this ball."

Ted let the **b**_____ go. Sandy ran to get it.

He **t**_____ the **b**_____ back to Ted.

Then Sandy held out his **p**_____ . Ted and Sandy shook hands.

"That's the way Sandy can **t**_____ !" said Ted.

Here's Sandy.

"Sights of the City," 81–93 • Teachers' Edition, 145–157

Introducing the Page: Ask pupils to comment on ways in which animals communicate. For example, birds chirp, bees buzz, cats purr. Relate pupils' comments to this page.

Additional Activity: Have pupils illustrate the way in which they might persuade Sandy to "talk."

44   Phonemic analysis: /ɔ/**aw** Structural analysis: **alk**, **all**, **and**, **ook**

Can You Pick the Word?

Find the word that belongs on the line, and write it.

_____

"Sights of the City," 81–93 • Teachers' Edition, 145–157

Introducing the Page: Have pupils read from the chalkboard they're, they'll, can't, don't, isn't. Help them recall the term contractions. Have pupils name the two words which make up each contraction on the chalkboard. Write them.

Additional Activity: Have pupils write sentences using they'll, I'm, can't, you'll, we'll.

1. When Ted _____ at school, he rides his bike.

   isn't

   don't

2. Carlo said, " _____ be outside."

   I'm

   I'll

3. Bozo is asking why _____ not at the fair.

   they're

   I'll

4. If _____ small, you will fit in the seat.

   you're

   you'll

5. Lucy and Donna _____ at school.

   aren't

   they'll

6. Dad said, " _____ going on here?"

   Can't

   What's

7. Dan and Don said, " _____ brothers!"

   We're

   We'll

8. Jen says that Jack _____ going.

   I'll

   isn't

9. _____ meeting Sam and Kay.

   They're

   They'll

Structural analysis: Contractions ending in **'re**, **'ll**, **n't**, **'s**, **'m**

45

Where Are They?

Write the letter for the word that belongs in the sentence.

a. over   **b.** in   **c.** on   **d.** under   **e.** next to

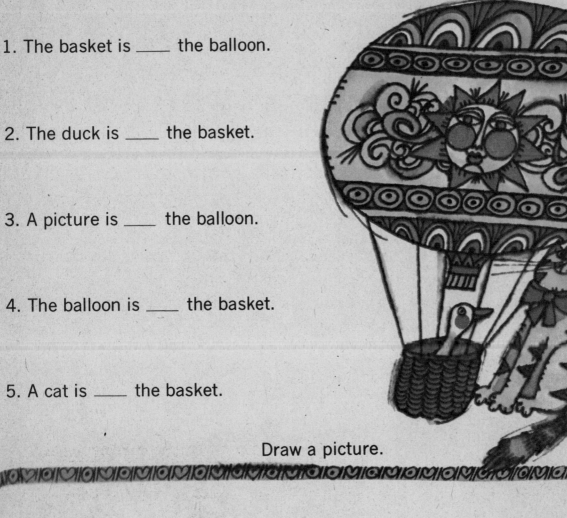

1. The basket is ____ the balloon.

2. The duck is ____ the basket.

3. A picture is ____ the balloon.

4. The balloon is ____ the basket.

5. A cat is ____ the basket.

Draw a picture.

1. Make a jet in the sky.

2. Make a boy under a tree.

3. Draw a kite flying over the boy.

4. Put a dog on the grass next to the boy.

Syntactical understanding: Understanding and using prepositions

"Sights of the City," 81–93 • Teachers' Edition, 145–157
Introducing the Page: Help the children with the first set of directions. For the second set of directions, explain to pupils that they are to draw all four items in the same scene rather than draw four separate scenes.

Smiles and Smiles

Read the poems and the questions. Write the answers on the lines.

We have 2 mice
Named Jigs and Jice.
One eats figs,
The other eats rice.

1. What are the mice named? _____ _____

2. Who do you think eats figs? _____

3. Who do you think eats rice? _____

I'll race
To the place
Where Grace
Sells lace,
And warm my face
At her fireplace.

1. What does Grace sell? _____

2. What will get warm at the fireplace? _____

"Snow," 95–99 • Teachers' Edition, 159–165

Introducing the Page: Have pupils read the two poems aloud. Help pupils read the words questions, poems.

Additional Activity: Let pupils try creating their own poems. They may write about Jigs and Jice, Grace's place, or a topic of their own choosing.

Phonemic analysis: Correspondence /s/c before e

Reading and Thinking

Read this story and answer the questions.

The small ant worked all day.

He wanted to get food for his children.

The ant could see the snow coming down.

The grasshopper didn't work.

He wanted to play and hop about.

He didn't get food for his children.

1. Who was the good worker?

_____

_____

2. Why did the grasshopper's children have no food?

_____

_____

_____

_____

3. Underline the sentence that tells why the ant wanted to get food for

   his children.

4. What do you think will happen to the grasshopper's children?

_____

_____

Literal and inferential comprehension: Recalling story details, inferring sequence

"Snow," 95-99 • Teachers' Edition, 159-165
Introducing the Page: Help pupils read the words questions, story, happen. Suggest that some pupils tape the questions and answers if there are tape recorders available.

More Reading and Thinking

Read this story and answer the questions.

It was Saturday, and the snow was white and pretty.

Ted and Pat put on boots and played in the snow.

They made a big snowman.

Mr. Migs came along with the mail.

He waved to the boys.

"Here you are," he said.

"The first snow-mailman!" said the boys.

1. Who made the snowman?

_____

_ _

_____

2. Why weren't the boys at school?

_____

_ _

_____

_ _

3. What did Mr. Migs have?

_____

4. What do you think Mr. Migs will do next?

_____

_ _

_____

_ _

Literal and inferential comprehension: Recalling story details, inferring sequence

"Snow," 95–99 • Teachers' Edition, 159–165

Introducing the Page: Help pupils read the words story, questions, and answers if tape recorders are available.

Some pupils may tape the questions and answers if tape recorders are available.

Additional Activity: Pupils may illustrate their responses to question 4.

Can You Do What the Words Say?

Draw 2 pictures.   You may add more to the pictures if you like.

Draw a bus coming down a street.   Make many children walking in the snow.
Put pretty flakes of snow everywhere.

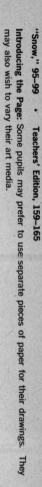

Make a lumberman in a big red truck.   Make six tall green trees.
Put red tags on four of them.

"Snow," 95–99 • Teachers' Edition, 159–165
Introducing the Page: Some pupils may prefer to use separate pieces of paper for their drawings. They may also wish to vary their art media.

Locational skills: Reading for specific information

The Jet Comes In

Read the story. Circle the answers to the questions.

___

The red and gray jet landed.

A man waved a light. The jet came to a stop.

A little truck took bags off the jet.

Many people came out of the jet.

1. Who helped the jet land?

   a little truck

   a man with a light

   the bags

2. In what way was the truck a help?

   it came down

   it came out of the jet

   it took bags off the jet

3. Where did the jet come from?

   the city

   the country

   the story didn't say

4. What was inside the jet?

   many people

   red and gray instruments

   a little truck

Literal and inferential comprehension: Recalling and inferring story details

"The New Fence," 100–104 • Teachers' Edition, 166–172
Introducing the Page: Help pupils read the words questions, story.

Think about These Sentences

Underline the right sentence.

1. Dan saw the sights of the city.

   The sights of the city saw Dan.

2. 5th Street came to a tall man.

   A tall man came to 5th Street.

3. Jets take off into the blue sky.

   The blue sky takes off in a jet.

4. A new fence didn't want Barry.

   Barry didn't want a new fence.

5. The snow was soft and white on the trees.

   The trees were soft and white on the snow.

6. The seesaw liked having the boys.

   The boys liked having the seesaw.

7. There's a man that can fix the fence.

   There's a fence that can fix the man.

8. Pat and Barry walked around to the back of the house.

   The back of the house walked around to Pat and Barry.

"The New Fence," 100–104 • Teachers' Edition, 166–172

Introducing the Page: Some pupils may need help with the first exercise.

Additional Activity: Pupils may illustrate one or more of the correct responses.

Syntactical understanding: Developing sentence sense

Things You Know

Make an **X** before every ending that could be right.

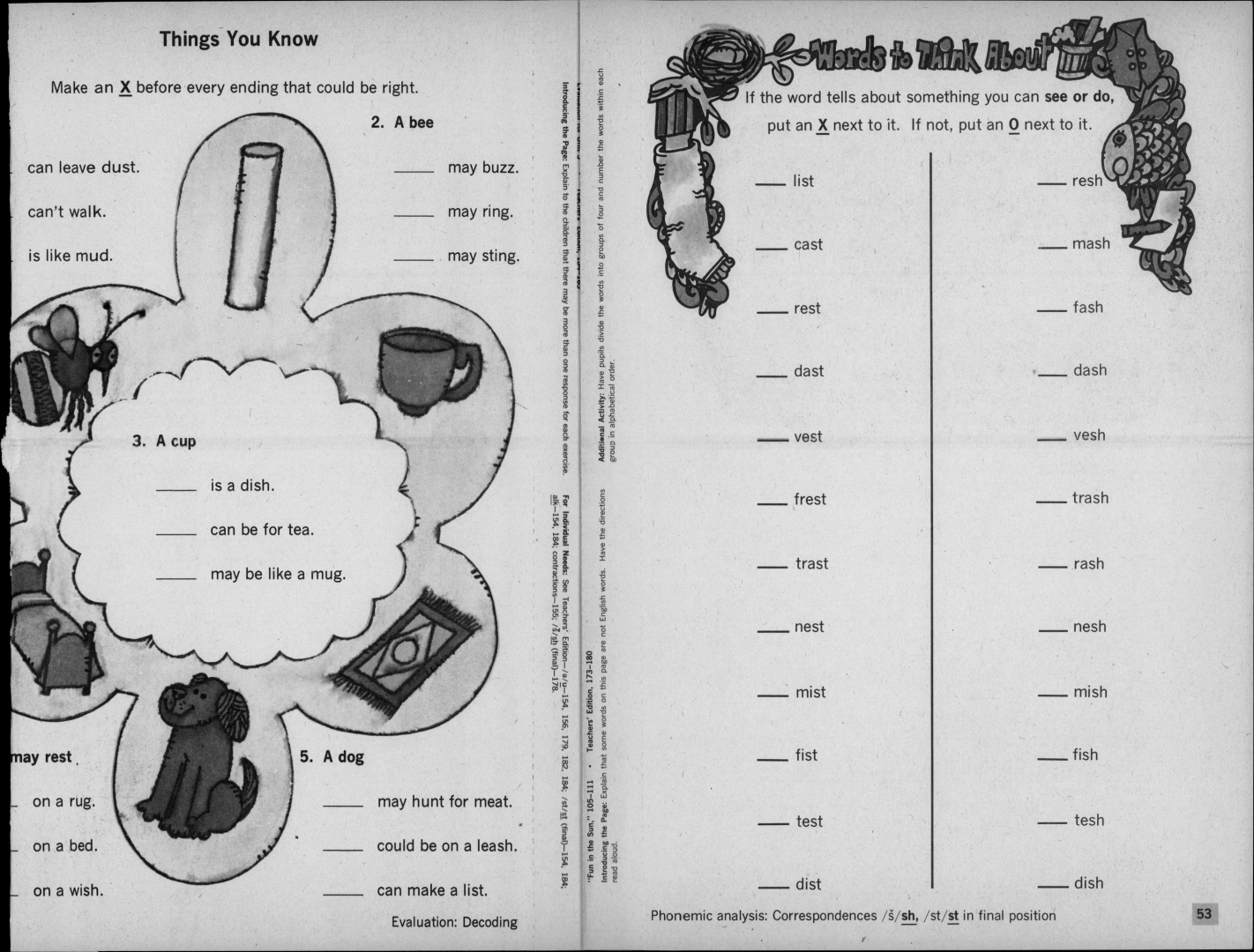

can leave dust.

can't walk.

is like mud.

2. A bee

_____ may buzz.

_____ may ring.

_____ may sting.

3. A cup

_____ is a dish.

_____ can be for tea.

_____ may be like a mug.

may rest

on a rug.

on a bed.

on a wish.

5. A dog

_____ may hunt for meat.

_____ could be on a leash.

_____ can make a list.

Evaluation: Decoding

Evaluation for Units 9 • Teachers' Edition, 107-109

Introducing the Page: Explain to the children that there may be more than one response for each exercise.

Additional Activity: Have pupils divide the words into groups of four and number the words within each group in alphabetical order.

For Individual Needs: See Teachers' Edition—/a/u—154, 156, 179, 182, 184; /st/st (final)—154, 184; alk—154, 184; contractions—155; /š/sh (final)—178.

"Fun in the Sun," 105-111 • Teachers' Edition, 173-180

Introducing the Page: Explain that some words on this page are not English words. Have the directions read aloud.

Words to Think About

If the word tells about something you can **see or do**, put an **X** next to it. If not, put an **O** next to it.

___ list	___ resh
___ cast	___ mash
___ rest	___ fash
___ dast	___ dash
___ vest	___ vesh
___ frest	___ trash
___ trast	___ rash
___ nest	___ nesh
___ mist	___ mish
___ fist	___ fish
___ test	___ tesh
___ dist	___ dish

Phonemic analysis: Correspondences /š/**sh**, /st/**st** in final position

What's the Opposite of Up?

Read the word. Then draw a line to the word that has the opposite meaning.

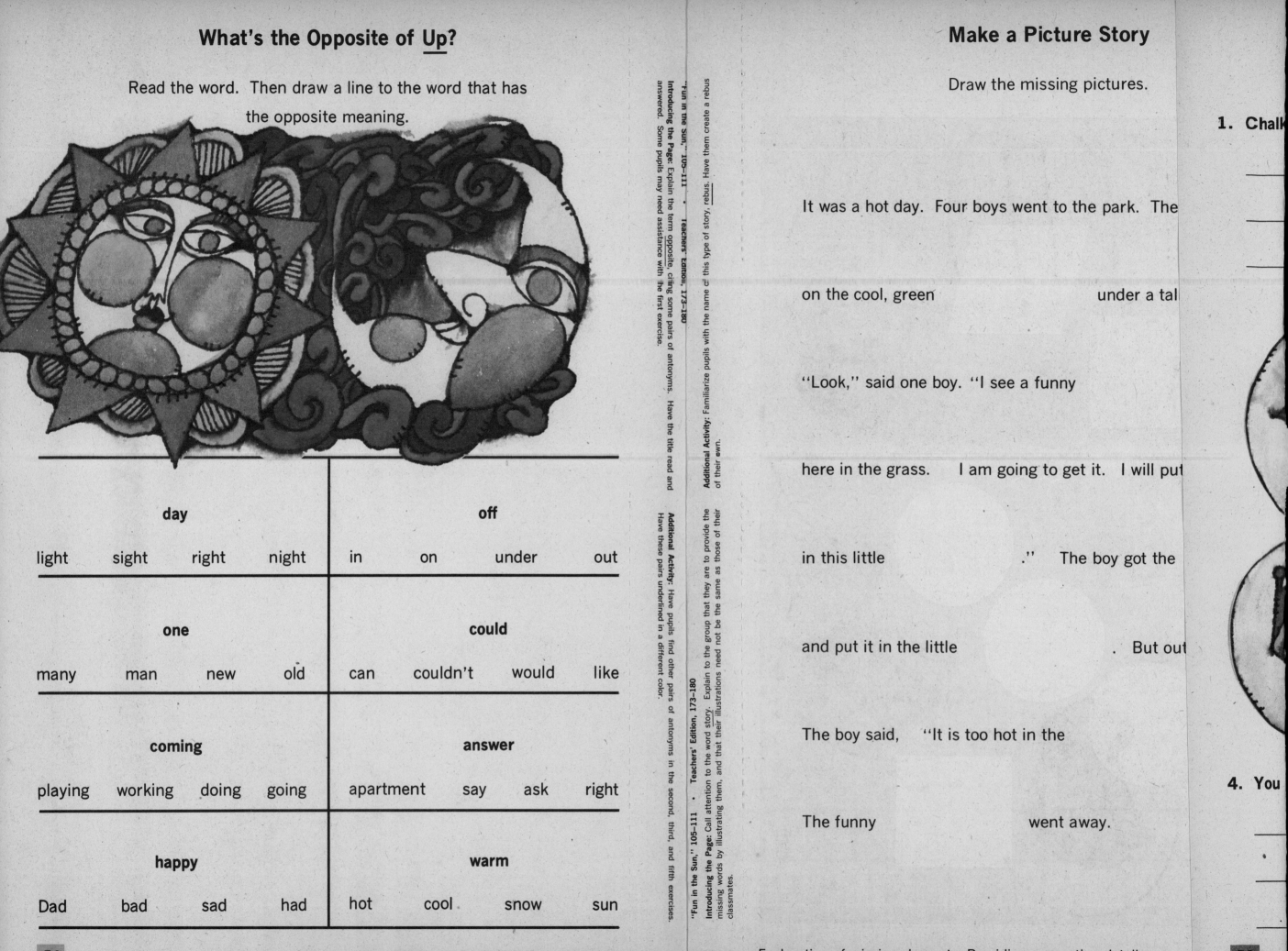

day				off			
light	sight	right	night	in	on	under	out

one				could			
many	man	new	old	can	couldn't	would	like

coming				answer			
playing	working	doing	going	apartment	say	ask	right

happy				warm			
Dad	bad	sad	had	hot	cool	snow	sun

"Fun in the Sun." 105–111 • Teachers' Edition, 173–180

Introducing the Page: Explain the term opposite, citing some pairs of antonyms. Have the title read and answered. Some pupils may need assistance with the first exercise.

Additional Activity: Have pupils find other pairs of antonyms in the second, third, and fifth exercises. Have these pairs underlined in a different color.

Additional Activity: Familiarize pupils with the name of this type of story, rebus. Have them create a rebus of their own.

"Fun in the Sun." 105–111 • Teachers' Edition, 173–180

Introducing the Page: Call attention to the word story. Explain to the group that they are to provide the missing words by illustrating them, and that their illustrations need not be the same as those of their classmates.

Make a Picture Story

Draw the missing pictures.

1. Chalk

It was a hot day. Four boys went to the park. The

on the cool, green   under a tal

"Look," said one boy. "I see a funny

here in the grass.   I am going to get it.   I will put

in this little   ."   The boy got the

and put it in the little   . But out

The boy said,   "It is too hot in the

The funny   went away.

4. You

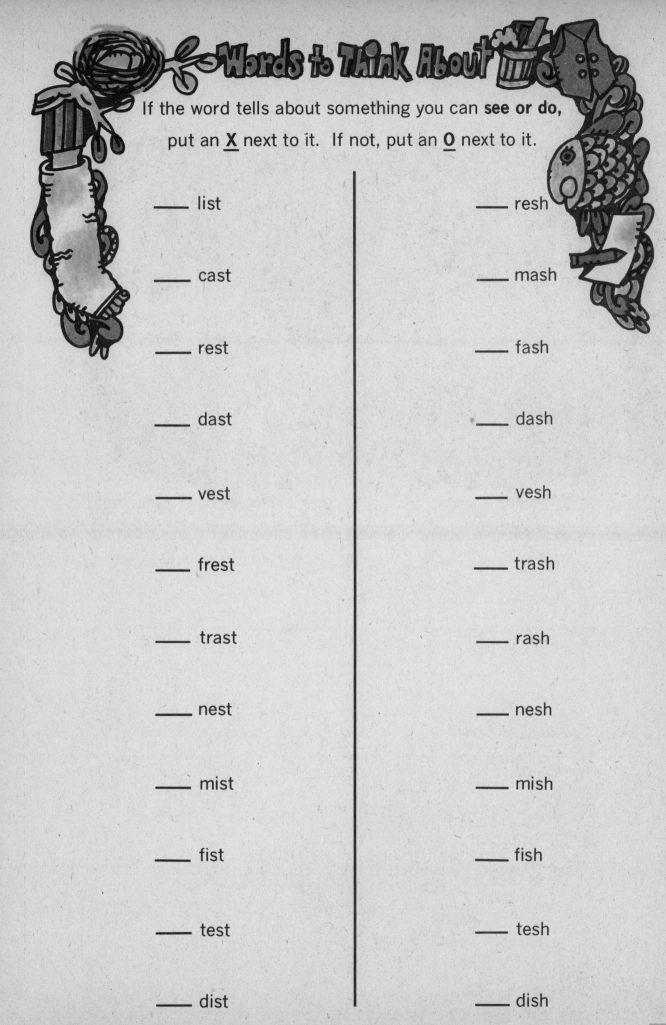

Words to Think About

If the word tells about something you can **see or do**,
put an **X** next to it. If not, put an **O** next to it.

____ list	____ resh
____ cast	____ mash
____ rest	____ fash
____ dast	____ dash
____ vest	____ vesh
____ frest	____ trash
____ trast	____ rash
____ nest	____ nesh
____ mist	____ mish
____ fist	____ fish
____ test	____ tesh
____ dist	____ dish

Phonemic analysis: Correspondences /š/**sh**, /st/**st** in final position

What's the Opposite of <u>Up</u>?

Read the word. Then draw a line to the word that has
the opposite meaning.

day				**off**			
light	sight	right	night	in	on	under	out
one				**could**			
many	man	new	old	can	couldn't	would	like
coming				**answer**			
playing	working	doing	going	apartment	say	ask	right
happy				**warm**			
Dad	bad	sad	had	hot	cool	snow	sun

Word meaning: Identifying antonyms

"Fun in the Sun," 105–111 • Teachers' Edition, 173–180

Introducing the Page: Explain the term opposite, citing some pairs of antonyms. Have the title read and answered. Some pupils may need assistance with the first exercise.

Additional Activity: Have pupils find other pairs of antonyms in the second, third, and fifth exercises. Have these pairs underlined in a different color.

Make a Picture Story

Draw the missing pictures.

It was a hot day. Four boys went to the park. They sat

on the cool, green   under a tall   .

"Look," said one boy. "I see a funny

here in the grass.   I am going to get it.   I will put it

in this little   ."   The boy got the

and put it in the little   . But out it jumped.

The boy said,   "It is too hot in the   ."

The funny   went away.

"Fun in the Sun," 105–111 • Teachers' Edition, 173–180

Introducing the Page: Call attention to the word story. Explain to the group that they are to provide the missing words by illustrating them, and that their illustrations need not be the same as those of their classmates.

Additional Activity: Familiarize pupils with the name of this type of story, rebus. Have them create a rebus of their own.

Exploration of missing elements: Providing supporting details

Things You Know

Make an **X** before every ending that could be right.

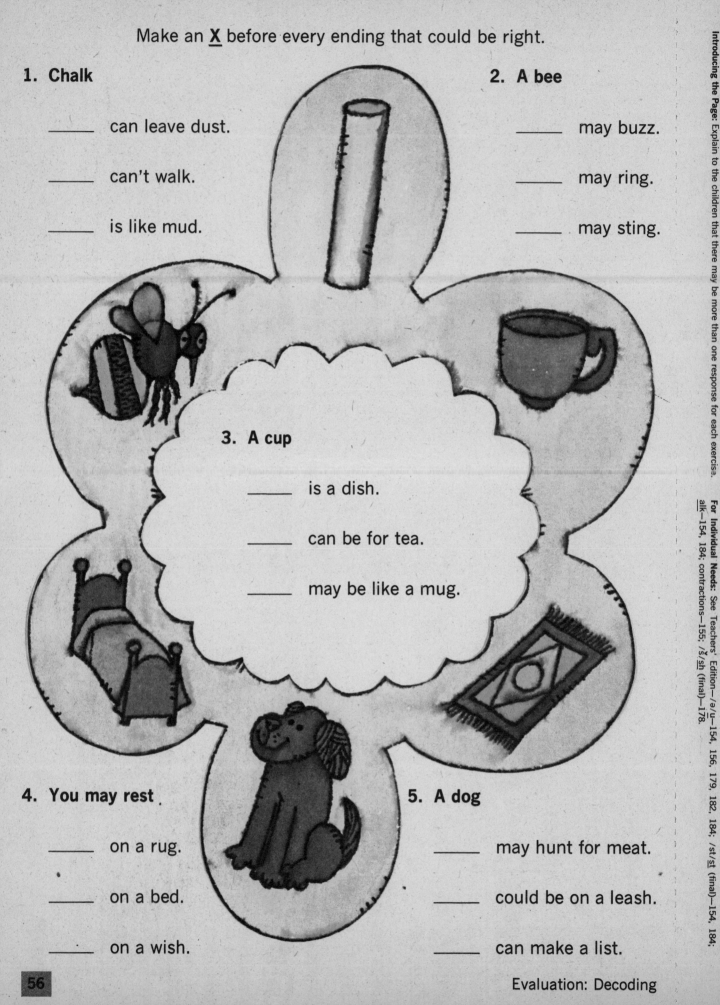

1. Chalk

_____ can leave dust.

_____ can't walk.

_____ is like mud.

2. A bee

_____ may buzz.

_____ may ring.

_____ may sting.

3. A cup

_____ is a dish.

_____ can be for tea.

_____ may be like a mug.

4. You may rest

_____ on a rug.

_____ on a bed.

_____ on a wish.

5. A dog

_____ may hunt for meat.

_____ could be on a leash.

_____ can make a list.

Evaluation: Decoding

Evaluation for Unit 3 • Teachers' Edition, 184–185

Introducing the Page: Explain to the children that there may be more than one response for each exercise.

For Individual Needs: See Teachers' Edition—/a/u—154, 156, 179, 182, 184; /st/st (final)—154, 184; alk—154, 184, contractions—155; /ŝ/ sh (final)—178.

All About Workmen

Read the story.

Workmen do many things to help people.

They can fix a fence or fix the TV.

They can put things on the boats in the harbor.

Workmen can fix a bus or a car.

They can take away the snow in big trucks.

Workmen help us day and night in the city and in the country too.

Find a word from the story to put here.

_____

Workmen help _____ .

_____

They can fix a _____ .

_____

Workmen work on _____ in the harbor.

_____

Workmen take away snow in big _____ .

_____

Workmen help us day and _____ .

Evaluation: Literal Comprehension

For Individual Needs: If any children have difficulty recognizing and recalling the story details, go over with them the sentences which were completed incorrectly. Meet with pupils on an individual basis.

Evaluation for Unit 3 • Teachers' Edition, 184–185

Think about These Words

Match the opposites. The first one has been answered for you.

Evaluation for Unit 3 • Teachers' Edition, 184–185
Introducing the Page: Help pupils with the directions.

1. **morning**   _____ leave

2. **cool**   **1** night

3. **happy**   _____ inside

4. **stay**   _____ sad

5. **outside**   _____ warm

_____

1. **coming**   _____ going

2. **bad**   _____ mine

3. **more**   _____ good

4. **yours**   _____ near

5. **far**   _____ less

For Individual Needs: To prepare additional activities for those children who had difficulty recognizing and understanding the words included in this activity, refer to the word list on pages 238–239 in the pupil's text for a complete list of the words introduced in Unit 3.

58   Evaluation: Vocabulary Development

Write the answers on the lines.

joke	rope	rose	bone
pole	stove	hose	hole

Don't fall into me.

I may be quite deep.

_____

I am a _____ .

I can make people laugh.

I am funny.

_____

I am a _____ .

I'm like a stick.

You may go fishing with me.

_____

I am a _____ .

I am red and pretty.

I smell good too.

_____

I am a _____ .

If you have a dog,

you may feed me to him.

_____

I am a _____ .

If you put me all around a big box,

I will keep the box from opening.

_____

I am _____ .

You may cook on me.

I am in your house.

_____

I am a _____ .

You need me to water the grass.

I can help put out a fire too.

_____

I am a _____ .

Phonemic analysis: Correspondence /ow/ <u>o_e</u>

Pick a Word!

Read the sentences. Write the words that go on the lines.

1. Andy is going _____ the telephone _____ .

who   **booth**   **to**

2. Miss White asked _____ would _____ the work.

do   **soon**   **who**

3. There will _____ be more to _____ .

soon   **who**   **do**

4. Carlo walked _____ the _____ .

do   **to**   **school**

5. If you want _____ see Ben, go to the _____ .

to   **pool**   **soon**

6. _____ lost a _____ ?

Who   **boot**   **too**

Phonemic analysis: Correspondences /uw/o, /uw/oo

"Night Light," 116–121 • Teachers' Edition, 188–197

Introducing the Page: Help pupils with the first exercise.

Additional Activity: Have pupils arrange words under book and too, according to the sound represented by the letters oo: cook, boot, hood, soon, food, took, pool, school, shook, booth, cool.

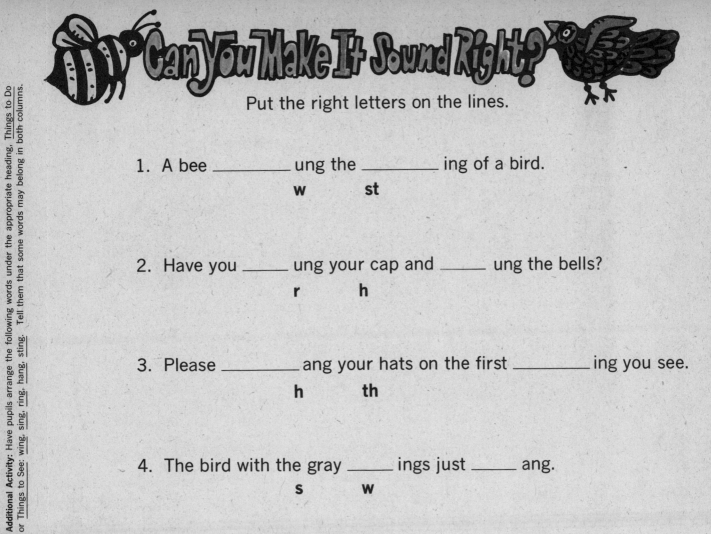

Can You Make It Sound Right?

Put the right letters on the lines.

1. A bee _____ ung the _____ ing of a bird.
           w   st

2. Have you _____ ung your cap and _____ ung the bells?
           r   h

3. Please _____ ang your hats on the first _____ ing you see.
           h   th

4. The bird with the gray _____ ings just _____ ang.
           s   w

5. The boys and girls will _____ ing while the bells _____ ing.
           r   s

6. A bee may _____ ing, but he can't _____ ing.
           st   s

7. The bee _____ ung the hand with the _____ ing on it.
           r   st

8. The _____ ing of the jet did not _____ ang into the wall.
           w   b

Structural analysis: Graphemic bases **ing**, **ang**, **ung**

It's Puzzle Time

The words for the puzzle are in the box. Read the sentences.

Then write in the missing letters.

"Mr. Harvey's Hat," 122–129 • Teachers' Edition, 198–208

Introducing the Page: Review the procedure for solving a crossword puzzle. Pupils may refer to puzzles which have already appeared in the Skills Handbook.

black

blackbird

blink

blame

blaze

bleed

ACROSS

1. This is another word for **fire**.

3. It can fly.

DOWN

1. You do this when you wink both

eyes at the same time.

2. If you get a bad cut, you will do this.

4. This is how the night can look.

Phonemic analysis: Correspondence /bl/ **bl**

Can You Match the Word with the Picture?

Underline the word that tells about the picture.

cap

lace

farm

safe

dart

lark

walk

chart

chalk

quack

harm

cart

mark

march

wash

jar

log

car

arm

trap

case

start

star

stack

trace

mark

pan

hard

card

trap

Phonemic analysis: Correspondence /ar/**ar**

Think about It

Find the word that fits the sentence. Write the letter in the blank.

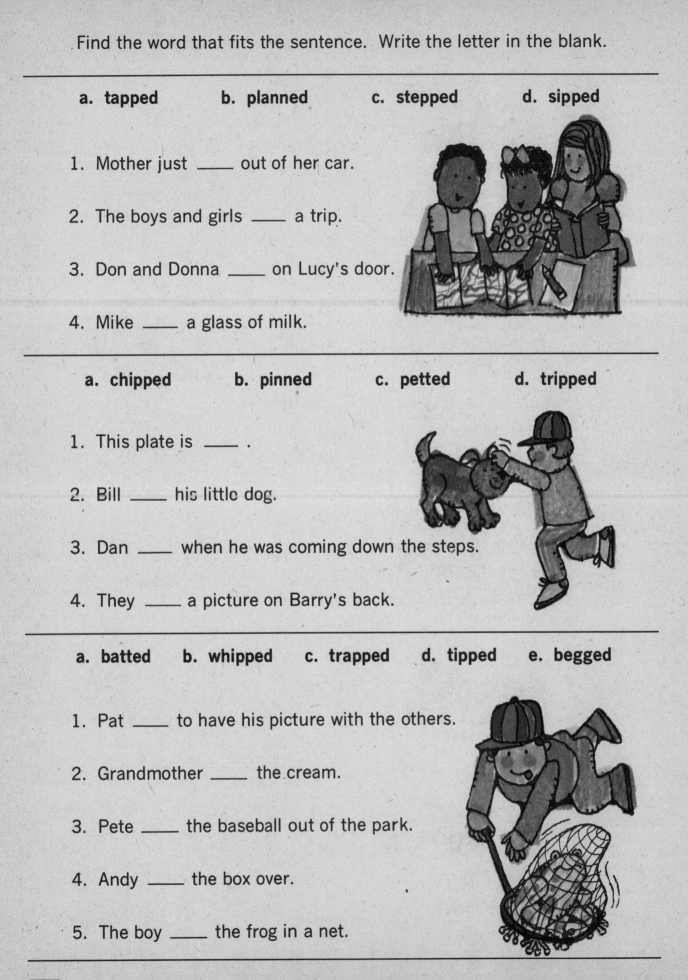

a. tapped   b. planned   c. stepped   d. sipped

1. Mother just ___ out of her car.

2. The boys and girls ___ a trip.

3. Don and Donna ___ on Lucy's door.

4. Mike ___ a glass of milk.

---

a. chipped   b. pinned   c. petted   d. tripped

1. This plate is ___ .

2. Bill ___ his little dog.

3. Dan ___ when he was coming down the steps.

4. They ___ a picture on Barry's back.

---

a. batted   b. whipped   c. trapped   d. tipped   e. begged

1. Pat ___ to have his picture with the others.

2. Grandmother ___ the cream.

3. Pete ___ the baseball out of the park.

4. Andy ___ the box over.

5. The boy ___ the frog in a net.

Structural analysis: Verbs with the final consonant letter doubled before **ed**

"Mr. Harvey's Hat," 122-129 • Teachers' Edition, 198-20■

Introducing the Page: Write hopped and napped. Point out the CVC spelling pattern of the root words and the doubled final consonant before ed. Review briefly the inflections d and ed.

Additional Activity: Have pupils write sentences using the following words: stopped, napped, dipped.

Can You Hear the Word parts?

Read the words. How many parts do you hear? If you hear one part, write **1** on the line before it. If you hear more than one part, write **X** on the line.

_____ face   _____ wasn't   _____ sun

_____ around   _____ us   _____ grandfather

_____ milk   _____ smoke   _____ many

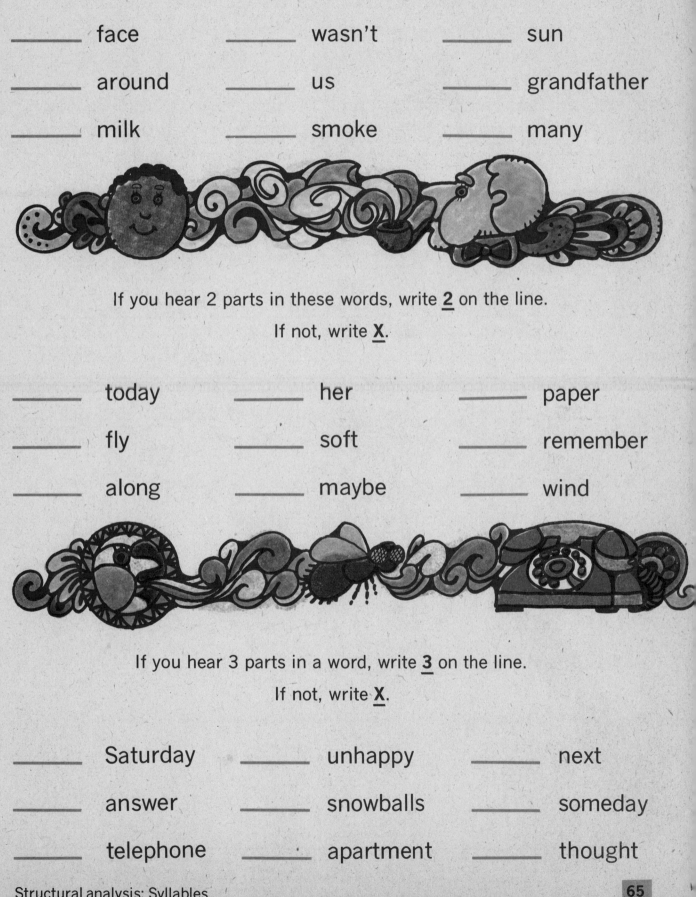

If you hear 2 parts in these words, write **2** on the line.

If not, write **X**.

_____ today   _____ her   _____ paper

_____ fly   _____ soft   _____ remember

_____ along   _____ maybe   _____ wind

If you hear 3 parts in a word, write **3** on the line.

If not, write **X**.

_____ Saturday   _____ unhappy   _____ next

_____ answer   _____ snowballs   _____ someday

_____ telephone   _____ apartment   _____ thought

Structural analysis: Syllables

Additional Activity: Have pupils circle all the words on the page in which they hear two word-parts.

"The Little Boy with the Big Name," 130–133 • Teachers' Edition, 209–214

What Is Missing?

Circle the word that is best for the sentence.

1. A dog and a duck and a _ _ _ _ _ _ _ _ _ _ _ lived in a blue box.

   bird   **cut**   **park**

2. The dog wanted to get something to _ _ _ _ _ _ _ _ _ _ _ .

   think   **eat**   **answer**

3. The dog asked the bird to _ _ _ _ _ _ _ _ _ _ him.

   chop   **mail**   **help**

4. The bird and the dog _ _ _ _ _ _ _ _ _ _ the duck in the blue box.

   waved   **left**   **talked**

5. The duck was _ _ _ _ _ _ _ _ _ _ .

   unhappy   **tall**   **seven**

6. Draw a picture of what you think the duck will do.

"The Little Boy with the Big Name," 130–133 • Teachers' Edition, 209–214
Introducing the Page: Do the first example with the group.

Inferential comprehension: Inferring supporting details, predicting outcomes

Make an **X** in the right box. Some words may have more than one **X**.

	things to do	things to see	places to go
fly			
trucks			
fence			
barn			
hat			
apartment			
eat			
letters			
sleep			
country			
laugh			
school			
swim			
airport			
owl			

"The Little Boy with the Big Name," 130–133 • Teachers' Edition, 209–214

Introducing the Page: Have the directions read aloud. Be sure that pupils understand that some responses may belong in more than one column. In this activity the literal comprehension skill of classifying ideas is also reinforced.

Additional Activity: Have pupils illustrate only those terms which indicate things to do.

Word meaning: Classifying words by definition

How Many Things?

If an underlined word tells about **more than one** thing, write **m** on the line.

If it tells about **one** thing, write **1** on the line.

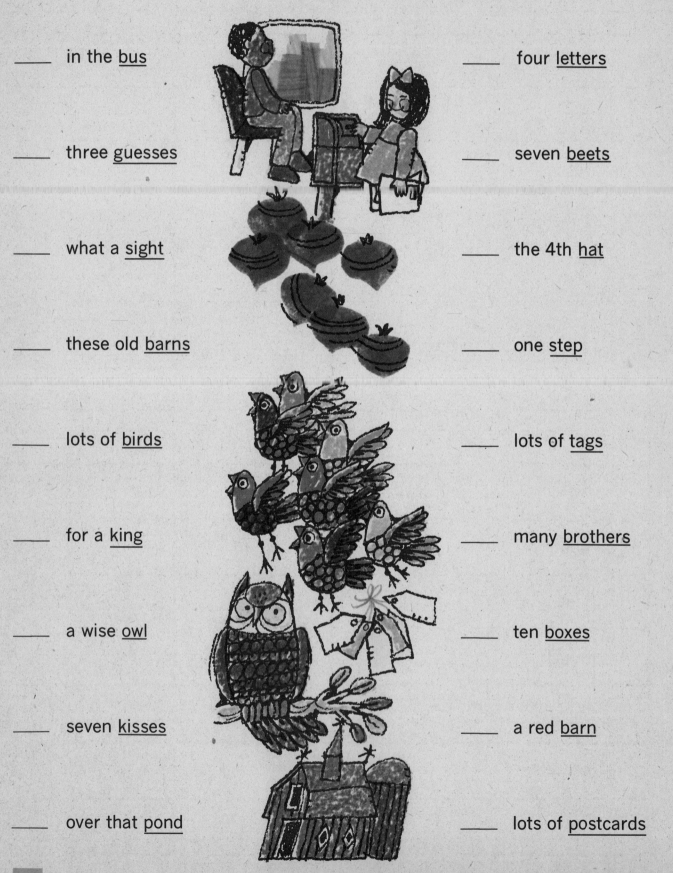

_____ in the <u>bus</u>

_____ three <u>guesses</u>

_____ what a <u>sight</u>

_____ these old <u>barns</u>

_____ lots of <u>birds</u>

_____ for a <u>king</u>

_____ a wise <u>owl</u>

_____ seven <u>kisses</u>

_____ over that <u>pond</u>

_____ four <u>letters</u>

_____ seven <u>beets</u>

_____ the 4th <u>hat</u>

_____ one <u>step</u>

_____ lots of <u>tags</u>

_____ many <u>brothers</u>

_____ ten <u>boxes</u>

_____ a red <u>barn</u>

_____ lots of <u>postcards</u>

"Three in a Tree," 135–142 • Teachers' Edition, 216–221

Introducing the Page: Some children may need assistance with the first examples.

Additional Activity: Have pupils write original sentences using at least three of the phrases.

Structural analysis: Plurals with **s** and **es**

Following Directions

When you were little, people had to read to you.

Now you can read many, many things without help.

You can read books, and you can read directions.

Here are some directions you can read. Do what they tell you.

Make an **X** on the box.

Draw a circle around the cat.

Underline the boy's name.

Make a check next to the thing that swims.

Write your name in the blank.

_____

- -

My name is _____

Underline this sentence: **I see flakes of snow.**

Word meaning: Understanding direction words

A Puzzle about Paddy

The words for the puzzle are here.   The sentences tell you about the words.

Write the answers in the puzzle.

fly

over

wings

far

from

penguin

mountain

ACROSS

1. Paddy wanted to _ _ _ _ _ _ _ _ _ _ .

2. The jet was _ _ _ _ _ _ _ _ _ _ away.

4. Paddy was King of the _ _ _ _ _ _ _ _ _ _ .

DOWN

1. Paddy walked away _ _ _ _ _ _ _ _ _ _ the other penguins.

3. The bird had no _ _ _ _ _ _ _ _ _ _ .

5. He walked _ _ _ _ _ _ _ _ _ _ a hill of snow.

m o u n t a i n

"Paddy the Penguin," 143–152 • Teacher's Edition, 225–234

Introducing the Page: Review with pupils the procedure for solving a crossword puzzle.

Additional Activity: Pupils may wish to make their own representations of Paddy. Aside from paint or crayons, other media, such as clay or papier-mâché, may be used.

Word meaning: Solving a crossword puzzle

How Will the Sentences End?

Finish the sentences. Underline the best ending.

1. Paddy liked to play _ _ _ _ _ _ _ _ _ _ .

at the other penguins   **with the other penguins**

to the other penguins

2. Another penguin pushed Paddy _ _ _ _ _ _ _ _ _ _ .

down the mountain   **for the mountain**

with the mountain

3. One penguin was _ _ _ _ _ _ _ _ _ _ .

with the top of the mountain   **to the top of the mountain**

on the top of the mountain

4. Paddy looked up _ _ _ _ _ _ _ _ _ _ .

with the blue sky   **into the blue sky**

down the blue sky

5. Paddy was in the blue sky _ _ _ _ _ _ _ _ _ _ .

in the mountains   **to the mountains**

over the mountains

6. Paddy was King _ _ _ _ _ _ _ _ _ _ .

from the penguins   **under the penguins**

of the penguins

"Paddy the Penguin," 143-152 • Teacher's Edition, 223-234

Introducing the Page: Have the directions read aloud. Some children may need help with the first exercise.

Additional Activity: Have pupils write sentences using one of the two remaining responses in each of the exercises.

Syntactical understanding: Completing sentences with prepositional phrases

Which Word Will Finish the Sentence?

Fill in the missing word.

Who   **bones**   **bloom**   **dark**

Roses _____ .

Nights can be _____ .

Dogs like _____ .

_____ are you?

---

bark   **rope**   **rung**   **note**

Jump _____ .

The bell had _____ .

Dogs _____ .

Write a _____ .

---

fang   **deep**   **bleed**   **mark**

Hit the _____ .

Holes can be _____ .

Cuts _____ .

A _____ is a sharp tooth.

Evaluation: Decoding

Evaluation for Unit 4 • Teachers' Edition, 237–238

For Individual Needs: See Teachers' Edition—/ow/o-e—193, 235, 237; /uw/o—193, 204, 214, 237; ing, ang, ung—193; /bl/bl—204, 235; /ar/ar—204, 224, 235, 237; ing.

Finish These, If You Can

Check the sentence that finishes each story best.

1. Three birds sang a song.

   They sang till they woke Father.

   _____ **Father was unhappy.**

   _____ **Father pushed Jack's car.**

2. The farmer's hat blew off in the wind.

   It landed on top of a stoplight.

   _____ **A blackbird took the hat.**

   _____ **Mother laughed at the dog.**

3. A blackbird lived on the side of an old building.

   One day some men came to take down the building.

   _____ **The man played a trick on Jeff.**

   _____ **Soon the blackbird looked for a new home.**

4. My pet owl is an unhappy owl.

   He wants to read the paper.

   _____ **A farmer raked the leaves.**

   _____ **How can an owl know how to read?**

5. My grandfather's friends play games with me.

   They read to me too.

   _____ **Could there be another boy as happy as I am?**

   _____ **Could there be another boy with wings?**

For Individual Needs: Meet individually with pupils who have difficulty predicting outcomes. As an aid to locating the source of a pupil's difficulty, have him read aloud any exercises that were missed.

Evaluation for Unit 4 • Teachers' Edition, 237–238

Introducing the Page: Have the directions read aloud.

Write the Answers

Find the words that go on the lines.

I come before four.

_____

I am _____ .

I am in the country and animals live in me.

_____

I am a _____ .

People say I am a wise old bird.

_____

I am an _____ .

You write on me every day.

_____

I am _____ .

We help birds and airplanes fly.

_____

We are _____ .

I can sing in a tree.

_____

I am a _____ .

bird

three

barn

owl

wings

paper

Evaluation: Vocabulary Development

Evaluation for Unit 4 • Teacher's Edition, 237-238

For individual needs: So that other activities may be prepared for remaining recognition and understanding of new words, refer to the list of new words for Unit 4 on page 239 of the pupil's text.

Riddles, Riddles, Riddles

Pick the word that goes on the line. Write on the line
the letter that comes before the word.

a. **Charles**	d. **jar**	g. **card**	j. **charm**
b. **Harvey**	e. **hard**	h. **dark**	k. **star**
c. **bark**	f. **car**	i. **farm**	

1. Find a word that ends the same as **harm.**

   A farmer works there. _____

2. Find a word that ends the same as **yard.**

   It means <u>not soft</u>. _____

3. Find a word that ends the same as **star.**

   You take jam out of it. _____

4. Find a word that starts the same as **car.**

   You can mail one. _____

5. Find a word that ends the same as **far.**

   You can ride in one. _____

6. Find a word that starts the same as **chart.**

   It's the name of a boy. _____

7. Find a word that ends the same as **mark.**

   A dog may do this. _____

8. Find a word that ends the same as **bar.**

   You'll find one in the sky. _____

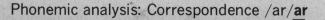

Phonemic analysis: Correspondence /ar/**ar**

"Building a Road," 156–159 • Teachers' Edition, 241–247
Introducing the Page: Help pupils read the word riddle. Some pupils may require assistance with the first exercise.
Additional Activity: Pupils may illustrate five of the words at the top of the page.

Could That Be Real?

Some things could be real, and some things just couldn't be.

If these things could be real, make an **X** under **COULD BE REAL.**

If not, make an **X** under **COULDN'T BE.**

THINGS	COULD BE REAL	COULDN'T BE
1. a newspaper that makes pancakes		
2. little rocks under big rocks		
3. some sand in a sand box		
4. a truck that rides on a fence		
5. a road made of candy		
6. an upside-down tree		
7. a newspaper with no words in it		
8. schools that walk		
9. men that work		
10. new roads		
11. a ship that helps build a road		
12. a house that jumps up and down		

Improbabilities entertained: Distinguishing reality from fantasy

"Building a Road," 156–159 • Teachers' Edition, 241–247

Introducing the Page: Some children may require assistance with the first two exercises.

Additional Activity: Have pupils illustrate two or more of the following phrases: schools that walk, a road made of candy, a truck that rides on a fence, a house that jumps up and down.

Get Set, Go!

Find the word that is missing from the sentence, and write it on the line.

touch	dish	each	peach
teach	fresh	leash	Which

_____

1. Did Bill _____ his dog that trick?

_____

2. I picked a _____ off the tree.

_____

3. Lucy wants a _____ for her food.

_____

4. Ben became sad _____ time Dad went away.

_____

5. Don't _____ the things in Mr. King's store.

_____

6. Is this milk _____ ?

_____

7. _____ balloon did Andy take?

_____

8. The policeman said you have to put a _____ on your dog.

Phonemic analysis: Correspondences /č/**ch**, /š/**sh** in final position

77

Additional Activity: Pupils may alphabetize the words in the first row, then the words in the second row across the top.

"The Other Side of the Mountain," 160–175 • Teachers' Edition, 248–264

Introducing the Page: Remind pupils that no word may be used more than once.

Find the Best Name

Put an **X** next to the best name for each set of sentences.

You may play tricks with words. Think about **sheet**. You may write on a **sheet** of paper. You can sleep on a **sheet** too. Words can mean more than one thing.

What would be a good name for this set of sentences?

_____ **A Sheet of Paper**

_____ **Words May Mean Many Things**

_____ **Bedtime**

I let Jack take my books to read. Sometimes he keeps them too long. I don't know what to do about it.

What would be a good name for this set of sentences?

_____ **Long Books**

_____ **Books Are Fun**

_____ **What to Do about Jack**

My brother Jeff just got his first car. He worked for the money to pay for it. He says he will take me for rides in his new, white car.

What would be a good name for this set of sentences?

_____ **My First Car**

_____ **Let's Go for a Ride!**

_____ **My Brother's Car**

Inferential comprehension: Finding the main idea of a paragraph

The Other Side of the Mountain, 180–175 • Teacher's Edition, 240–204
Introducing the Page: Explain to the children that each set of sentences needs a title. Tell them that they are to pick the title from among the choices listed.

Additional Activity: Have pupils write a paragraph for one of the remaining titles.

Now You Can Write

Pick the word that goes with each picture. Write it.

road   machine   workers

mountain   rocks   cap

truck   trees   sun

Think Before You Write!

Pick the word that goes in the blank.

Write the letter on the line.

1. Dad _____ the ice.   **a. zipped   b. chipped**

2. Ben is tired; he is _____ .   **a. napping   b. trotting**

3. Mike _____ the tree last year.   **a. petted   b. trimmed**

4. Butch _____ over the glass.   **a. pinned   b. tipped**

5. Pete was just _____ his dog.   **a. petting   b. chipping**

6. The boys aren't _____ the game.   **a. sipping   b. winning**

Write the root word on the line. The first answer is here for you.

1. begged   beg

2. pinned

3. petted

4. ripped

5. sipping

6. winning

7. tipping

8. zipping

Structural analysis: Verbs with the final letter doubled before **ed** or **ing**

Introducing the Page: Although most pupils can decode the word root, it might be helpful to review the significance of the term. This activity also reinforces the ability to identify the root word in inflected verbs.

What's in the Newspaper?

Read the news in this newspaper. Fill in the missing words.

BOY WILL GO TO THE MOON

_____

- - - - - - - - - - - - - - - - - - -

A boy named _____ is on his way to the moon.

_____

- - - - - - - - - - - - - - - - - - -

Three men are going to the _____ with

_____

- - - - - - - - - - - - - - - - - - -

Scot. They took off in a tall _____

_____

- - - - - - - - - - - - -

The blast-_____ was at nine this morning.

_____

- - - - - - - - - - - - - -

It will take a long _____ to get to the moon.

When Scot gets back, we will

ask him to write about

_____

- - - - - - - - - - - - - - - -

his _____

moon   **trip**

Scot   **time**

rocket   **off**

Inferential comprehension: Inferring supporting details

Take Your Pick

Find the part that finishes the sentence. Write **1** or **2** or **3** in the blank.

He stopped at each house _____ .

1. in the sand at the beach

Which balloon _____ ?

2. popped

Children were digging _____ .

3. on his way

Do they teach swimming _____ ?

1. off the tree

I picked a peach _____ .

2. is running away

Which boy _____ ?

3. at your school

Evaluation: Decoding

Evaluation for Unit 5 • Teachers' Edition, 284–286

Introducing the Page: Have the directions read aloud by one of the pupils.

For Individual Needs: See Teachers' Edition—/č/ch (final)—260, 278.

Match Sentence Parts

Which ending is best for each sentence? Write the letter on the line.

Men need to plan _____ .

a. put the tar on the road

He watched the men as they _____ .

b. but I can't remember the dream

I know I dreamed _____ .

c. where they will build a road

Tom ate part of the cake _____ .

a. they go in a rocket

When men go to the moon, _____ .

b. from that place near the road

Did you carry the dirt _____ ?

c. before the cake was ready

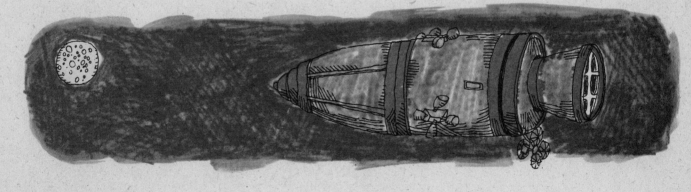

You have tar _____ .

a. all over your coat

I wish _____ .

b. as it rolled along

I saw the car _____ .

c. summer would come

Evaluation: Language Development

For Individual Needs: To help the pupil determine his need for further help with syntactical understanding, have the mismatched sentence parts read aloud by the pupil. Then suggest that he try other combinations of sentence segments until he finds a combination which makes sense to him. Meet with pupils individually.

Evaluation for Unit 5 • Teachers' Edition, 284–286

Introducing the Page: Have one of the pupils read the directions aloud.

Which Word Is Right?

Put the right letter in each blank.

You can sit on _____ ,

but you put on _____ .

a. rocks

b. socks

You can ride in a _____

on a road topped with _____ .

a. tar

b. car

A farmer's fat _____

always likes to _____ .

a. pig

b. dig

Birds like to _____

in the treetops in _____ .

a. spring

b. sing

Don't take a _____

when you have on your _____ .

a. nap

b. cap

I like to _____

of lots of ice _____ .

a. cream

b. dream

A bird can _____

up into the _____ .

a. fly

b. sky

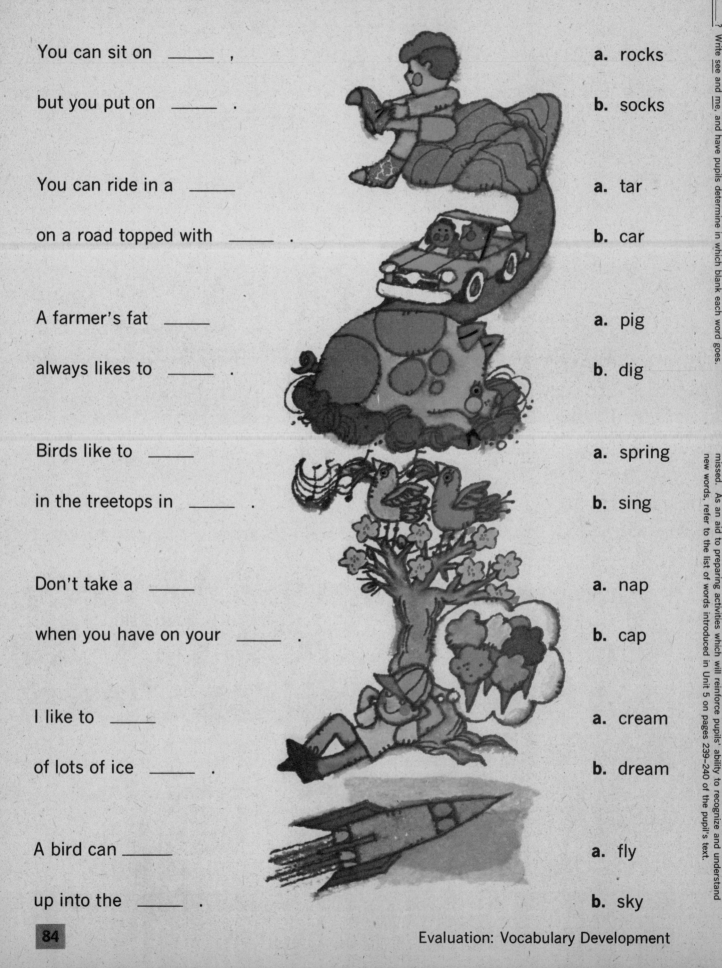

Evaluation for Unit 5 • Teacher's Edition, 284–286

Introducing the Page: Write the following lines, one below the other: What do you _____ ? Write see and me, and have pupils determine in which blank each word goes.

For Individual Needs: Meet with each pupil individually and have him read aloud any exercises that were missed. As an aid to preparing activities which will reinforce pupils' ability to recognize and understand new words, refer to the list of words introduced in Unit 5 on pages 239–240 of the pupil's text.

Evaluation: Vocabulary Development

Here's Another Puzzle!

You will find the words for the puzzle in the box.   Read the hints under the puzzle.   Write the letters in the right boxes in the puzzle.

chalk

wink

wall

sink

sting

sing

stand

stall

rink

ACROSS

2. You do this if you don't sit.

4. A bee can do this.

5. It is fun to write with this.

6. It's the side of a house.

DOWN

1. You run hot water into it.

2. If you feel happy, you may do this.

3. You may find ice here.

4. This is a place in a barn for animals.

Structural analysis: Graphemic bases <u>ink</u>, <u>all</u>, <u>alk</u>, <u>ing</u>, <u>and</u>

Additional Activity: Pupils may write sentences using the words which they used in the puzzle.

Introducing the Page: Pupils may wish to refer to earlier puzzles in the Skills Handbook as a review of the procedure to be followed in completing a crossword puzzle.

Something Isn't Right

Read each set of four words. One word will not belong in each set.

Circle that word.

birthday	Saturday	dream	today
four	wish	seven	three
mountain	pond	lake	sea
woods	logs	sawmills	shoes
warm	hot	cool	telephone
walk	watch	look	see
gingerbread	milk	pork chops	money
school	rocket	jet	kite
apartment	barn	house	tar
elephant	noise	lion	dog
newspapers	books	workers	signs
leaves	winter	spring	summer
red	wind	blue	green

Inferential comprehension: Classifying according to inferred relationships

"The Elves and the Shoemaker," 192-201 • Teacher's Edition, 250-301

Introducing the Page: Ask pupils which of the following words does not belong: Christmas, Halloween, Thanksgiving. Relate their response to this page. Introducing the Page: apartment.

Additional Activity: Have pupils mark, with numbers 1, 2, or 3, the number of syllables in each word. Pork chops should be treated as two words.

Have You Ever Lost a Pal?

You have not seen all of these words before.   See if you can read the story and underline the answers to the questions.

The boy walked down the path. He was looking down as he walked. Then he saw the girl with her dog. He thought about his dog.

The girl didn't say a word. She saw that the boy was not happy. He didn't want to talk.

Then he smiled at her. She smiled back. Soon he would feel fine.

The boy bent down and petted the girl's dog. He thought of his dog again.

Then he said, "Someday I'll get another dog."

1. What is a good name for the story?

   The Sad Boy   **The Happy Boy**

2. Where did the boy walk?

down the road   **down the path**

3. How did the boy feel?

   not happy   **not sad**

4. What was the boy thinking about?

      his dog   **his school**

5. Why was the boy sad?

   He had lost his owl.   **He had lost his dog.**

Phonemic and structural analysis: Reviewing decoding with known word elements

Phonemic Activity: Ask pupils if they have ever lost a pet or a cherished possession. Have them write about it or have them write a story pretending that they have lost something of value.

The Best Name

Make an **X** next to the best name for each set of sentences.

Pets don't have to be dogs or cats.   My friend has a turtle for a pet.   I have four pet fish.   A boy in the country could have a duck or a hen for a pet.

What would be the best name for this set of sentences?

_____ **My Friend's Pets**

_____ **Pets in the Country**

_____ **All Kinds of Pets**

There is magic in ice and snow.   There is magic in cars and boats.   It's magic to turn on the TV and see people and animals.   Magic isn't just at fairs.   Magic isn't all tricks and games.   Magic is all around me.   It's all around you too.

What would be the best name for this set of sentences?

_____ **Happy and Sad**

_____ **Magic All Around**

_____ **I Like TV**

Kay has three plants.   She gives them water three times a week.   She turns them around every day so that they get the light.   Sometimes she turns the dirt over and over in the plants.   That way they can take air into their roots.   Kay's plants are green and fresh all the time.

What would be the best name for this set of sentences?

_____ **Turning Plants**

_____ **Kay Keeps Plants Green and Fresh**

_____ **Kay**

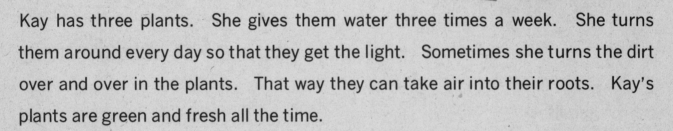

Inferential comprehension: Finding the main idea of a paragraph

Introducing the Page: Remind pupils of Skills Handbook page 78 on which they selected the most appropriate title for different sets of sentences. Explain that they will be doing the same on this page.

Words Can Be Pictures

Write the words that go on the lines. Then draw pictures of your answers.

money   **horses**   **shop**   **coat**

elves   **shoes**   **roof**

something to
keep you warm

animals that
you may ride

a place where you
get new things

magic people

what people may
save in a bank

what you put
on your feet

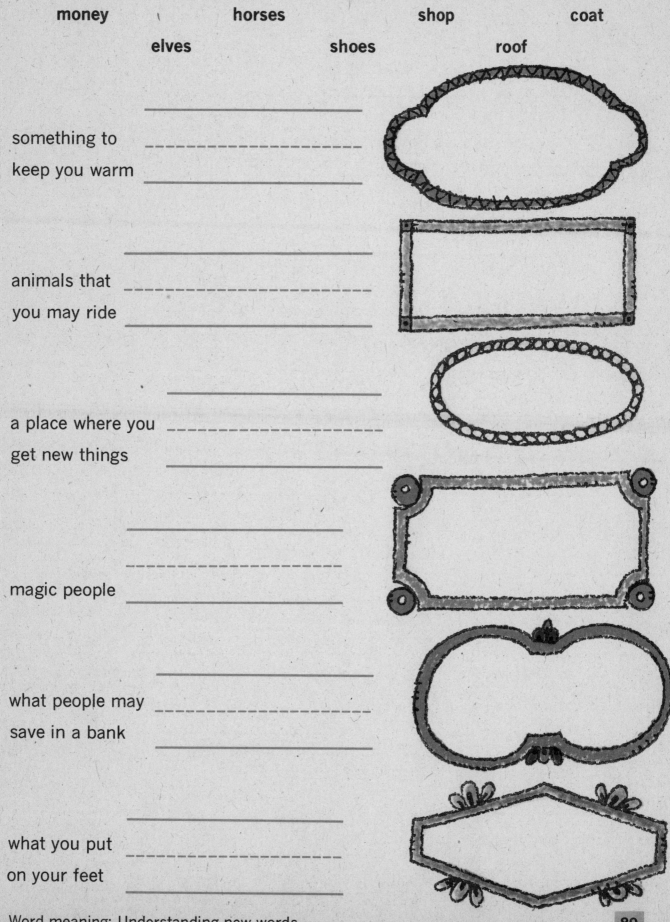

Word meaning: Understanding new words

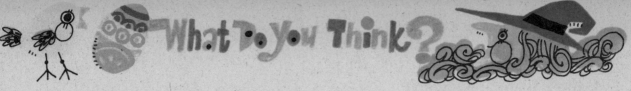

Answer the question with **yes** or **no**. Put an **X** in the right place.

	YES	NO
1. Could people make a fire with a match?		
2. Does Mother stitch your socks?		
3. Can you pitch a baseball?		
4. Have you ever seen a witch do her tricks?		
5. Would you like to eat a batch of pancakes?		
6. Do you know a boy named Mitch?		
7. Does a chick hatch from an egg?		
8. Did you ever fall into a ditch?		
9. Is there a patch on your play pants?		
10. Can you hitch a horse to a tree?		

90

Phonemic analysis: Correspondence /č/tch

Introducing the Page: Ask pupils: Do you like milk? Can you swim? Do you have red socks? Point out that their answers varied. Explain that answers may also vary in the activity which they are about to do.

How about Horses?

Some horses still run wild in this country, but some horses do not.

There are people who like to ride horses just for fun.   Some people have horses to do farm work.   Other people like to race horses.

Make pictures of 2 things that horses may do.

Literal comprehension: Recalling story details

Who Is It?

Find the best word for each sentence.   Write **a** or **b** in the blank.

White Horse, ZZZ-ZZZ

Introducing the Page: Write: Do _____ have your paper? I need _____ coat today. Beside the sentences write: a. my. b. I. Have the sentences and responses read. Help pupils write in the blanks the letters which correspond to the appropriate responses.

1. The elves helped the little old man and the little

    old woman by making shoes for _____.

    a. them   **b. your**

2. The beautiful white horse ran so fast that no one

    could catch _____.

    a. we   **b. him**

3. The boy had sheep, and the wolf ate _____.

    a. them   **b. your**

4. The Indians liked to catch horses. _____ liked to

    ride the horses too.

    a. He   **b. They**

5. Have you ever played tricks on _____ friends?

    a. your   **b. him**

6. The elves had new red coats. _____ liked their

    new red coats.

    a. Their   **b. They**

Syntactical understanding: Supplying pronouns in specific sentence context

More Words to Think About

Find the word that goes on the line. Write it.

watch   That dog _____ at me!

winked   Dan put his _____ on the sink.

pink   Lucy put a _____ patch on her coat.

think   Ann didn't _____ the ball.

match   Your socks don't _____ each other.

catch   I like to _____ about my friend Mitch.

patch   Jeff lost the _____ off his coat.

pitch   Read to us about the mean, old _____.

witch   Can you _____ the ball to me?

Introducing the Page: Have the directions read aloud. Explain that no response should be used more than once.

For Individual Needs: See Teachers' Edition—ink—298, 310, 326; /ch/tch (final)—318, 325.

The Magic of Elves

Read this story.

Wouldn't it be fun if we all had elves? Elves could give
your father a shave in the morning. They could cook
for your mother. Elves could play games with you.

Elves could ride on horses or in rockets. They could take you
over the mountains and to other lands. Elves could do work
just like magic.

Circle the answer to each question.

Who could do your work?

shaves   **elves**   **lands**

What could elves give your father?

a cook   **a rocket**   **a shave**

What could elves play?

games   **father**   **bus**

What could elves ride on?

mornings   **horses**   **games**

How would elves do work?

like mountains   **like morning**   **like magic**

Evaluation: Literal Comprehension

Introducing the Page: Point out that there are two sets of directions.

For Individual Needs: Meet individually with pupils who have had difficulty recognizing and recalling details. Have the story and any questions that were missed read aloud.

Things That Come in Pairs

There are many things that come in pairs.

Like shoes and socks. And hands and feet.

What other things come in pairs?

Draw some!

Introducing the Page: Write the word pair. Have pair read and its meaning explained. Relate pupils' comments to this activity.

For Individual Needs: Have pupils compare the results of their work. Such a comparison may help pupils who have been unable to think of many "pairs."

INDEX TO STRAND EMPHASES

COMPREHENSION

Inferential

Reinforcement
  Classifying according to inferred relation-
    ships: 86
  Deducing answers from descriptive clues:
    37
  Inferring the main idea of a paragraph: 78,
    88
  Inferring sequence: 16, 48, 49
  Inferring supporting details: 51, 66, 81
  Predicting outcomes: 22, 25, 66
Evaluation
  Deducing responses from specific clues: 41
  Predicting outcomes: 73

Literal

Reinforcement
  Classifying ideas: 12, 35
  Recognizing and recalling details: 4, 11,
    48, 49, 51, 91
Evaluation
  Recognizing and recalling details: 19, 57,
    94

CREATIVITY

Reinforcement
  Confrontation with uncertainties: 1
  Exploration of missing elements: 55
  Improbabilities entertained: 26, 76
Evaluation
  Considering multiple hypotheses: 95

DECODING

Reinforcement
  Phonemic analysis
    Consonant correspondences
      /bl/bl: 62
      /k/c: 6
      /s/c: 6
      /s/c before e: 6, 47
      /č/ch (initial): 15
      /č/ch (final): 77
      /s/c before i: 6
      /f/f (final): 33
      /gr/gr: 10
      /nd/nd: 27, 31
      /nt/nt: 31
      /š/sh (final): 53, 77
      /sm/sm: 5
      /st/st (initial): 10
      /st/st (final): 53
      /č/tch: 90
      /tr/tr: 10
    Vowel-consonant correspondence
      /ar/ar: 63, 75

Vowel correspondences
  /æ/a: 43
  /ɔ/a: 24
  /ɔ/aw: 24, 44
  /e/e: 43
  /i/i: 43
  /a/o: 23
  /ow/o: 8
  /uw/o: 8, 60
  /u/oo: 3, 32, 36
  /uw/oo: 32, 36, 60
  /ow/o_e: 59
  /ə/u: 43
  General review: 87
Structural analysis
  Compound words: 2
  Contractions: 45
  Graphemic bases
    alk: 44, 85
    all: 24, 27, 44, 85
    and: 27, 44, 85
    ang: 61
    ing: 61, 85
    ink: 85
    ook: 3, 27, 44
    ung: 61
  Root words and endings
    Plurals with s, es: 68
    Verbs with ed, d: 21
    Verbs with final consonant letter doubled
      before ed: 64, 80
    Verbs with final consonant letter doubled
      before ing: 80
  Syllables: 65
  General review: 87
Evaluation
  compounds, /u/oo, ook, /sm/sm, /s/c,
  /ow/o, /č/ch (initial): 18
  /ɔ/a, all, /a/o, /nd/nd, /nt/nt, /f/f (final),
    /uw/oo: 40
  /ə/u, /st/st (final), alk, contractions, /š/sh
    (final): 56
  /ow/o_e, /uw/o, ang, ung, /bl/bl, /ar/ar:
    72
  /č/ch (final): 82
  ink, /č/tch: 93

LANGUAGE

Language Development

Reinforcement
  Completing sentences with the appropri-
    ate phrase: 14
  Completing sentences with prepositional
    phrases: 71
  Developing sentence sense: 52

N O P 7
PRINTED IN THE UNITED STATES OF AMERICA